Welcome to London

1

Big Ben
© S. Wasek/age fotostock

Getting to London

BY PLANE

♿ *Airlines p. 150.*

From Gatwick
Airport – ✆0344 892 0322 - www.gatwickairport.com.
Gatwick Express (train) – 30min to Victoria Station- departures every 15 min - from £17,40 - www.gatwickexpress.com.
Thameslink (train) – 45min to Blackfriars (then St Pancras) - 24hr departures; 15min to 1hr - from £8 - www.thameslinkrailway.com.
Taxi – £80 to central london (1hr).

From Heathrow
Airport – ✆0844 335 1801 - www.heathrowairport.com.
Piccadilly Line (underground) – 50min to Piccadilly Circus - departures every 5 min - From £5.10 - www.tfl.gov.uk.
Heathrow Express – 15 min to Paddington station (connects to underground) - departs every 15 min - From £25 - www.heathrowexpress.com.
Taxi – 50-70 £ jusqu'au centre (50mn).

From London City
Airport – ✆020 7646 0088 - www.londoncityairport.com.
Docklands Light Railway (DLR) – 22min to Bank (connection with the metro) - departures every 8-15 min - From £4,90.
Taxi – £35 to central london.

From Luton
Airport – ✆01 582 4051 00 - www.london-luton.co.uk.
Train – *Shuttlebus* to Luton station (5pm-midnight; £2), take a train to King's Cross-St Pancras in 45min (connects to underground) - 24hr service, trains run 15min to 1hr - From £14.
Taxi – £90 to central london (1h15).

From Stansted
Airport – ✆0844 335 1803 - www.stanstedairport.com.
Stansted Express (train) – 45min to Liverpool Street - departures every 15min - From £19 - www.stanstedexpress.com
Taxi – £90 to central london (1hr15).

From Southend
Airport – ✆01 702 538 500 - www.southendairport.com.
Train – Approx. 50 min to Stratford, and Liverpool Street - departures every 30min - From £15,10 - www.abelliogreateranglia.co.uk.
Taxi – £90 to central london (1h15).

BY TRAIN

The **Eurostar** (♿ *p. 150*) arrives at St Pancras International.

3

River Thames from above, with the Houses of Parliament, Westminster Bridge, London Eye and Shard
© Jon Arnold/hemis.fr

♿ *See Public Transport p. 158.*

Unmissable
Our picks for must-see sites:

Big Ben and Westminster ★★★
Map E5-6 - 🚻 p. 14

National Gallery ★★★
Map E4 - 🚻 p. 21

British Museum ★★★
Map E3 - 🚻 p. 90

The Changing of the Guard at Buckingham Palace ★★★
Map D5 - 🚻 p. 25

The City ★★★
Map GH3-4 - 🚻 p. 48

Notting Hill ★★
♿ p. 82

The Tower of London ★★★
Map H4 - ♿ p. 58

South Kensington museums
Map AB6 - ♿ p. 76

5

The Queen's Walk ★★★
Tate Modern ★★★
Map FG4 - ♿ p. 60 and 64

Regent's Park ★★★
Map BC1-2 - ♿ p. 86

Our top picks

💙 **A walk along a London canal from Little Venice to Camden Lock**. Ideal for a sunny day, this walk starts in the Little Venice district, at the junction of Regent's canal and the Grand Union canal (⊖ *Paddington ou Warwick Avenue*) Stroll alongside colourful barges before crossing Regent's Park to Camden market, with its many bars and restaurants. The route can also be travelled by boat (www.londonwaterbus.com). *See p. 158*.

💙 **See a show in the West End**. London's answer to New York's Broadway is renowned for its excellent stage performances. For cheap tickets, head for the TKTS kiosk on Leicester Square (www.tkts.co.uk) or the theatre's box office the morning of the performance. See p. 141 and 180. Traditionalists may prefer to check out one of the plays shown at Shakespeare's Globe. *See p. 62*.

💙 **Bargain hunting in London's infamous street markets** On Fridays and Saturdays in Portobello (Notting Hill) and all week in Camden Town. The stalls and boutiques stock vintage clothing, antiques and various collectibles. *See p. 82 and 94*.

💙 **Dine in one of Brick Lane's many curry houses**. This quirky East End street is lined with a host of Indian restaurants. A spicy curry or chicken tikka masala will set the taste buds tingling ready for a quick browse round this hip area's vintage shops and Sunday's flea market. *See p. 101*.

💙 **End the day enjoying a beer in one of the city's historic pubs.** Hampstead in particular boasts various cosy drinking havens: some fitted out with leather benches, vast mirrors and antique woodwork; others packed full of bric-a-brac, old jukeboxes, candles and fireplaces. *See p. 128*

💙 **Partake in the British tradition of afternoon tea.** Around 4-5pm, many of the higher-end department stores and prestigious hotels in the capital lay on a top-notch spread including dainty sandwiches, perfect patisserie and delicious scones. *See p. 126 and 182*.

💙 **Break for lunch in the unique atmosphere of Borough Market.** London's oldest food market - dating back a thousand years. All manner of gourmet treats and ground-breaking chefs inhabit its hallowed halls. *See p. 61, 119 and 135*.

© carlosanchezpereyra/iStockphoto.com

Regent's Canal at Camden Lock

💚 **A tour of the National Portrait Gallery** to spot the faces of famous British figures from history. *See p. 22.*

💚 **Visit the Sir John Soane's Museum** to immerse yourself totally in this cabinet of curiosities – the historic home, museum and library of the distinguished architect. *See p. 44.*

💚 **Admire Harrods food halls,** an Art Nouveau palace of opulence and spectacle, with richly-packed displays of fancy food. *See p. 70 and 136.*

💚 **Get up high!** Climb to the top of the London Eye, the Shard, the Walkie Talkie building, St Paul's Cathedral or the glass walkway of Tower Bridge to admire the modern London skyline, from the stunning skyscrapers of the City to the banks of the Thames. *See p. 173.*

💚 **Wait until after dark to discover the big-hitters amongst London's museums:** The National Gallery (Fri until 9pm, p.21), the National Portrait Gallery (Thu-Sat 9pm, p.22), Tate Modern (Sat, p.64), the Victoria and Albert Museum (Fri until 10pm, p.76). Tate Britain (p.18) and the Natural History Museum (p.77) regularly organise themed evenings and candlelight visits are offered at Sir John Soane's Museum (p.44) and Dennis Severs' House.

London in 3 days

DAY 1

▶ Morning

Start your visit with a trip on the **London Eye ★★★** (p. 68) for a bird's eye view over the city. Book in advance to avoid queuing. Then visit **Westminster Abbey★★★** (p. 16) walking by **Big Ben★** and **Parliament★★★** (p. 14), **Whitehall★** (p. 19) and **St James's Park★★** (p. 24). If you can get to Buckingham Palace by 11.30am, hang around to watch the **Changing of the Guard★★★** (p. 24)

▶ Midday

Lunch at **Trafalgar Square★★** (p. 20), either in the crypt of St Martin-in-the-Fields church or at the National Gallery.

▶ Afternoon

After a short tour of the **National Gallery★★★** (p. 21), eyes up to see the lights of **Piccadilly Circus★** (p. 30), then eyes down to the shops along **Regent Street★★** (p. 32) and **Oxford Street★** (p. 84). Save some energy and cash for the big department stores which count London stalwarts Fortnum & Mason, Liberty, Hamleys and Selfridges among their number.

▶ Evening

Go for a drink in a traditional pub in **Covent Garden★** (p. 35) or **Chelsea★★** (p. 74. If you're after more excitement, head to **Soho★** (p. 32), with its numerous bars and clubs.

DAY 2

▶ Morning

On a Friday or Saturday, nothing beats a stroll around the flea market in **Portobello Road★** (p. 136) in **Notting Hill**. On Sunday, head to **Camden Locks★★** (p. 94) or the flower market in **Columbia Road** (p. 139), in the **East End** (⊖ Old Street), which is bordered by pretty shops and serves as a stepping stone to the markets of **Brick Lane★** (p. 140) and **Spitalfields★** (p. 139).

Tower Bridge

© Tetra Images/Photononstop

▶ *Midday*

Have lunch in Notting Hill, Cam[...]
Town or Brick Lane, to enjoy th[...]
hustle and bustle of weekend L[...]

▶ *Afternoon*

Go see the Egyptian mummies i[...]
the **British Museum**★★★ (p. 90)[...]
drop by The Rosetta stone, the E[...]
Island statues and the Parthenor[...]
friezes on your way round. Admir[...]
the treasures of the **British Librar**[...]
(p. 92) before going for a walk in [...]
newly rejuvenated neighbourhood[...]
of **King's Cross** (p. 92) or the
grounds of **Regent's Park**★★★
(p. 86) and its zoo. Other options:
one of the three museums in **South**
Kensington★★★ (p. 74), the **Wallac**[...]
Collection★★★ (p. 85) or the **Imperial**
War Museum★★★ (p. 69), across the
Thames.

▶ *Evening*

Start with a cocktail in the bar of a
grand Mayfair hotel, or at the top of
the Heron Tower (or the Oxo Tower,
p.119), where you can enjoy the view
by night. Head on to the bars and
clubs of Southwark, Shoreditch,
Clerkenwell, Brixton or Camden.

DAY 3

▶ *Morning*

For classical art, a visit to the **Tate**
Britain★★★ (p. 18) is an absolute
must. From there, hop on the river
shuttle to the **Tate Modern**★★★
(p. 64). Follow the banks of the
Thames towards **Shakespeare's**
Globe★★ (p. 62), and **Southwark**
Cathedral★★ (p. 62). Climb to the top
of the **Shard**★★ (p. 61).

[...]a relax in a deckchair.
Hire out a self-service bicycle, brunch
on a restaurant terrace, take a canal
*boat trip, follow the **Queen's Walk**★★★*
along the Thames, explore the
***Docklands**★ and the **Olympic Park**,*
or soak up the atmosphere of a flea
markets.

▶ *Midday*

Lunch at **Borough Market** (p. 61).

▶ *Afternoon*

Check out **City Hall** (p. 61), and cross
Tower Bridge★★ (p. 59) to visit the
Tower of London★★★ (p. 58). Take
a walk through the **City**★★★ (p. 48),
with its skyscrapers and old buildings
such as Leadenhall Market, footsteps
echoing in the deserted weekend
streets. Finish your afternoon with
a tour of **St Paul's Cathedral** ★★★
(p. 48) and afternoon tea.

▶ *Evening*

End your stay with a show in the West
End (p. 141 and 178).

Discovering London

Millennium Bridge and St. Paul's Cathedral
© Jon Arnold/hemis.fr

London today

Both eccentric and classic, chic and wacky, bold and anchored in its heritage, London has something to distract you.

Its cultural diversity is expressed in its colourful mosaic of neighbourhoods, its markets, where Londoners love to stroll at the weekend, and at vibrant festivals. London, in French is written with an "s" to emphasize its plurality. There is the Port of London, with its sandy docks, warehouses and cranes, Royal London, in red and gold, Westminster and Whitehall, London's cosmopolitan and bustling Brixton and Brick Lane, with its markets, cheap Bangladeshi restaurants and street vendors, London's festive Soho, Covent Garden and Camden, musicals and clubs. London's chic and old-fashioned Chelsea and Mayfair, with colonnaded patrician mansions, the historic Tower of London, London's bohemian Notting Hill, the City; London's administrative and financial centre where everyone wears white collars and grey suits.

Contrasted, immense and protean, London is also changing. You have to climb to the top of the Coca-Cola London Eye, the Shard or Walkie-Talkie (with its Sky Garden) to get a better understanding of the change in progress.

A horizontal city, with two or three-storey Victorian brick houses, with the help of futuristic skyscrapers, standing up like chess pieces in the heart of the City, in Canary Wharf and on the south bank of the Thames. Towers with nicknames such as 'The Gherkin', 'The Cheesegrater', 'The Walkie-Talkie' or 'The Scalpel', symbols of a new globalized metropolis, the first financial centre on the planet. The construction frenzy that has taken hold of London linked to the population boom (the population should increase from 8.3 million to 10 million by 2030), radically transforms the physiognomy of the urban landscape, sometimes triggering discontent. Whatever one thinks of it, it reveals an incredible vitality, proving that London is the opposite of a museum city!

In London, there is **Inner London**; the centre comprising 13 boroughs plus the City, and **Greater London** which includes 19 other suburbs. Each borough includes different areas with affirmed identities. It is at this level that we should look at the city.

The West End and the North

Soho and **Covent Garden** draw you into a whirlwind of nightlife and music halls. To the west and north of Piccadilly Circus are two of London's most famous thoroughfares; **Piccadilly** and Regent Street, which define upmarket **Mayfair**. North of it, **Oxford Street**, with its abundance of department stores will make you dizzy. From **Trafalgar Square**, where all gatherings take place, you will reach the institutional areas that stretch further south; **Westminster** Palace (Parliament) and its abbey, **Buckingham Palace** and the upmarket area of **St James's**. Further west, the upscale area of **Knightsbridge** known for its luxury shopping is dominated by the venerable Harrods. To the south, **Chelsea**, long appreciated by artists, has an equally distinguished look. Less elitist, but also elegant, **South Kensington** is home to some of London's greatest museums, such as the Victoria and Albert Museum. To the northwest of **Hyde Park**, the residential area of **Notting Hill** attracts the bohemian middle class with its village flair, alternative culture and trendy bars and restaurants. To the north, opulent **Marylebone** and beautiful **Regent's Park** offer pleasant surprises such as the magnificent Wallace Collection. More to the east, the formerly disreputed area of **King's Cross and St Pancras**, congested and centred on their monumental railway stations, has gradually regained its reputation.

Not far away, **Camden Town** takes advantage of its alternative neighbourhood image and the popularity of its markets. Further north, **Hampstead** and **Highgate**, separated by Hampstead Heath, a preserved heath with ponds left to nature. On the eastern edge of the West End, peaceful **Bloomsbury** and **Holborn** maintain their intellectual side thanks to the British Museum and the University of London.

The City, Yesterday and Today

A true historical centre of the capital, the City is today the economic heart. In the middle of new skyscrapers rises the Tower of London, one of the City's oldest monuments and Saint Paul's Cathedral. North of the City, Clerkenwell and Islington are now among the most "Boho" areas.

Reclaiming the East

The **East End**, a formerly poor area of working class London, including **Spitalfields**, Whitechapel, Shoreditch and Hoxton, is now one of the most popular places. Spitalfields, desirable and authentic, is the best place to find **vintage** and designer shops.

Revival along the River

Long ignored, the former industrial areas of **South Bank** and **Southwark** now embody modernity. Restored, these cultural and tourist sites make a beautiful walk along the Thames. There are many attractions including the Tate Modern, The Coca-Cola London Eye and The Shard. Further east, the old, refurbished **docks** stand alongside Canary Wharf's glass and steel towers. On the other side, **Greenwich**, known for its meridian, is a UNESCO World Heritage Site for its remarkable architecture. It's clear that a single weekend won't be enough to exhaust all the charms of this surprising and endearing city.

Westminster ★★★

Westminster's name evokes monarchical and political history. Coronations and other prestigious royal celebrations are held at Westminster Abbey, and the opening of the parliamentary sessions takes place at the palace. During state visits, royal personalities and dignitaries are accompanied by an impressive cavalry escort. The Houses of Parliament, of which Big Ben is the lighthouse, seduced Monet, who found an association between the changing subjects of the monument, the river and sky in one of his most famous oil painting series.

▶**Access:** ⊖ Westminster, Pimlico, Victoria.
Map of the area: p. 17. Detachable map E5-6-7.
▶**Tip:** Parliament is only open to the public during parliamentary holidays and on Saturdays for the rest of the year. Reserve your ticket in advance.

PALACE OF WESTMINSTER ★★★

(Houses of Parliament)
E5-6 Parliament Square -
⊖ *Westminster - ☎020 7219 4114 - www.parliament.uk/visiting - ♿ - Aug-Oct: Mon-Sat 9h-16h15 (summer intermission), rest of the year: Sat guided tour: £25.50 (child £11), audio tour: £18.50 (child £7.50).*
The ticket office is situated on the same level as Victoria Embankment.
In medieval times, the Kings of England expanded and decorated Edward the Confessor's palace, but most of the old buildings, which Parliament occupied later, were ravaged by the Great Fire in 1834. After the disaster, it was Charles Barry and Augustus Pugin who returned to renovate the palace, which became the Houses of Parliament. These architects provided London with a sumptuous neo-Gothic palace, a masterpiece of Victorian architecture that was completed in 1860. The building contains more than 1100 rooms, 100 staircases and 3km of corridors all representing a total area of 3.24 hectares.

Big Ben ★

The iconic Clock Tower was completed in 1859. The name originally referred to the huge bell (weighing 13.5t) in the 96m high tower. The light shining above the clock remains lit during sittings of the House of Commons.

Westminster Hall ★

Spared by the Great Fire of 1834, this great hall that William II added to the palace between 1097 and 1099 is the oldest building. Westminster Hall, where royal banquets were held in the Middle Ages, was transformed between 1394 and 1399. At that time, what was perhaps the most

Palace of Westminster and Lambeth Bridge

14

beautiful wooden **ceiling** of all time was constructed, a hammer beam roof designed by the king's master carpenter, Hugh Herland, adorned with flying angels.

House of Commons★
(The Commons Chamber)

Destroyed by a bomb in 1941 and rebuilt in 1950, the Commons Chamber is modestly decorated with a chair at the end of the chamber for the *speaker*. The government and the majority sit on the right, the opposition and shadow cabinet sit on the left of the speaker. The red lines along the two sides of the green carpet show the line that cannot be crossed by members of Parliament during debate.

16

House of Lords★★
(House of Peers)

Lavishly decorated in gold and scarlet red. The ornate gilded gothic throne occupied by the royal family on the day of the opening of the session, sits on a dais at the very end of the chamber. Under a gold ceiling divided into panelled compartments, benches are covered in red fabric and *woolsack*. The seat of the Grand Chancellor is reminiscent of the wool sacks on which the king's advisers formerly sat.

WESTMINSTER ABBEY★★★

E6 Parliament Square -
⊖ Westminster - ℘020 7222
5152 - www.westminster-abbey.org -
⅙ - abbey: Mon-Sat 9h30-15h30 (Wed
18h) - £20 (child £9) - audio guides

and brochures. The gardens are not open every day, check the calendar on the website.

Westminster Abbey, where William the Conqueror was crowned on Christmas Day 1066, was built by Edward the Confessor in Roman style. It was only after its reconstruction in 1220 under Henry III that it acquired its Gothic appearance. Henry III began by erecting the **Chapel of the Virgin Mary** to house the shrine of Edward the Confessor, canonized in 1163. It took more than two centuries to finish the building, with the completion of the Henry VII Chapel in 1503-1519, masterpiece of the Perpendicular Gothic style. The additions, like the western towers built in 1722-1745 designed by **Christopher Wren** and Nicholas Hawksmoor were made in the same Gothic style.

Interior- The vaults are splendid, the sculptures and carvings of the stalls and arches are delicate, often marvellous, sometimes humorous, the tombs in the Henry VII and St. Edward Chapels, as well as the radiant chapels, are solemn yet expressive. The arms of the transept and the aisles abound in carved monuments, especially the right semi-transept and its famous **Poets' Corner**★. It's in the area beyond the choir that the coronation ceremony takes place. On the right is a 16th century tapestry behind a large 15th century altar of rare beauty. A little further on, you can see an old ecclesiastical canopied seat whose remains are adorned with carved heads (Henry III, Edward I). The **Henry VII chapel**★★★, with its superb fan vaulted ceiling, is the

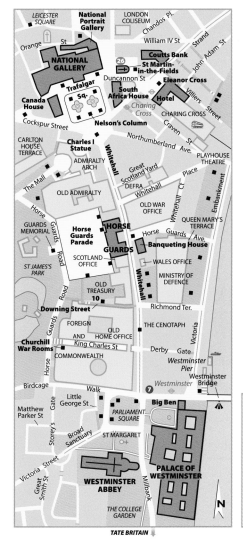

LEICESTER SQUARE

most beautiful of the many treasures in the abbey.
The banners of the Grand Cross Knights of the Order of the Bath still hang above the stalls, adorned with original 16th-18th century misericords and the coats of arms of their former occupants and squires.

In the **Chapel of Edward the Confessor★★** (*access only during a guided tour*), the shrine of the holy king is surrounded by the tombs of five kings and three queens. In the centre, leaning against a fence of carved stones (1441), is the **throne of the coronation** under which the **stone of Scone** lies.

Chapter House★★ dated between 1248-1253 is an octagonal room with ridge rib (lierne) and tierceron vaults descending on a central pier (pillar) to eight «Purbeck» marble columns. Its walls are partially covered with medieval paintings.

17

WESTMINSTER WHITEHALL TRAFALGAR

0	100 m
	100 yards

WHERE TO EAT

Café in the Crypt.................... 26

WHERE TO DRINK

St Stephen's Tavern.................. 7

© J. Arnold Images/hemis.fr

Main foyer staircase, Tate Britain

TATE BRITAIN★★★

*E7 Main Entrance: Atterbury St. -
⊖ Pimlico - ℘020 7887 8888 -
www.tate.org.uk - ♿ - 10h-18h (last
admission 17h15 for exhibitions) -
night themes (Late at Tate) certain
Fridays (calendar on website) - closed
24-26 Dec - free except temporary
exhibitions - restaurant, café.*

It was in 1891 that **Henry Tate**, a sugar
merchant and collector of modern
art donated his collection to the
nation and £80,000 to construct the
building.

The location of the former Millbank
Prison was offered by the government.
The Tate, opened its doors in 1897 as
a museum of modern British Art. Its
collection consisted not only of the
donor's collection, but also a large
number of paintings acquired by the
State since the creation of the National
Gallery (1824). Legally independent
from the National Gallery since 1955,
the Tate has renovated its buildings
and defined a new policy after the
opening of the Tate Modern in 2000
(♿ p. 64).

Dedicated to **British art from 1500
to the present day** the collections
present a chronological order that
allows you to see the evolution
of painting and recurring themes
according to the times. You will
discover the greatest British painters,
such as Reynolds, Hogarth, **Blake**,
Constable, Gainsborough, the Pre-
Raphaelites, Bacon, Freud, Hockney,
but also sculptures by both Henry
Moore and and Barbara Hepworth.
The Clore Gallery contains an
exceptional collection of works by
Turner.

Whitehall★ and Trafalgar Square★★

It is at this famous square known worldwide, with its popular statue, fountains and the National Gallery in the background, that Whitehall Avenue ends (beginning at the Palace of Westminster). Trafalgar Square serves as a forum for political rallies such as Christmas gatherings around the Christmas tree, or New Year's Eve while waiting for the sound of Big Ben's chimes at midnight.

▶**Access:** ⊖ Charing Cross, Westminster, St James's Park.
Map of the area p. 17. Detachable map E4-5.
▶**Tip:** Enjoy free admission to major national museums by staggering your visit and try not to see everything in a day.

WHITEHALL★

E5 ⊖ *Charing Cross or Westminster.*
The axis formed by Whitehall, (formerly called King Street) and Parliament Street is lined with official buildings. Whitehall is the district of executive power.

CHURCHILL WAR ROOMS★★

E5 Clive Steps, King Charles St. - ⊖ *Westminster or St James's Park -* ℘*020 7930 6961 - www.iwm.org uk -* ♿ *- 9h30-18h (last admission 17h) - closed 24-26 Dec - £19, audio guide included.*
The shelter that had been installed to protect Winston Churchill, his war cabinet, and the chiefs of staff from air strikes, was the Second World War headquarters.
The different rooms of this underground labyrinth, where hundreds of people lived has remained the same since 1945. There is a museum dedicated to Churchill, where you can discover the head of State and the man in his intimacy. The exhibition is organized around a gigantic interactive biography through the five major periods of his life; his youth (1874-1900), his political rise (1900-1929), the 1930s (1929-1939), the warlord (1939-1945) and the statesman during the Cold War (1945-1965).

DOWNING STREET

E5 ⊖ *Westminster.*
This famous street is lined with Georgian style houses. **No. 10** has

been the official residence of the Prime Minister since its construction by Robert Walpole in 1732.

BANQUETING HOUSE★★

E5 Whitehall - ⊖ *Charing Cross or Westminster* - ☎*020 3166 6154/5 - www.hrp.org.uk -* ♿ *- 10h-17h (last admission 16h30) - closed 1st Jan and 24-26 Dec (check the website for information on closures) - £6.50, audio guide included.*

The only surviving part of the Whitehall Palace (inhabited by the rulers until 1689) was made by **Inigo Jones** for James I in 1619. Outside, on the west side, there is a good view of the facade. Its elevation comprises columns with superimposed Ionic and Corinthian orders, surmounted by balusters. Jones brought his personal touch by omitting the traditional central door, which gives more majesty to it all. Inside, there's a very nice room with a golden balcony. Above, lavishly decorated beams divide the ceiling into compartments adorned with magnificent Rubens paintings (1634-1635).

HORSE GUARDS★★★

E5 Facing Banqueting House - ⊖ *Charing Cross or Westminster - changing of the guard: http:// changing-guard.com - Mon-Sat 11h, Sun 10h (see calendar on website) - parade on the Mall between Horse Guards and Hyde Park Barracks.*

With its central structure dominated by a clock tower and three arches, the regimental barracks built in the middle of the 18th century by **William Kent**, frame the courtyard where the ceremonies take place. The sentinels in front of the building confirm its role as an official entrance to Buckingham Palace. A crowd of tourists gathers every day to be photographed alongside these proud helmeted riders in silver armour on their beautiful horses dressed in black, but it is in vain that you try to get a smile!

TRAFALGAR SQUARE★★

E4 ⊖ *Charing Cross.*

Pedestrianized and dedicated to cultural or political events, this place, now a national symbol, remains the meeting place for major events. Completed around 1840, when Charles Barry levelled and built the north terrace of the National Gallery, it has been dominated by the famous **Nelson's Column** since 1842, consisting of a 4.5m high statue representing the grand admiral who lost his life winning the battle of Trafalgar.

At each of the four corners there is a plinth carrying one of the historic heros, except one which remained empty until 2005 due to insufficient funds.

Every two years the «**Fourth Plinth**» is used for a modern art sculpture. Next to Whitehall, the equestrian statue of Charles I was cast by Le Sueur in 1633. On the National Gallery's left facade is Canada House, a classic Bath stone building erected by Robert Smirke between 1824 and 1827.

© National Gallery, London

Detail of Sun rising through Vapour: Fishermen cleaning and selling Fish *(before 1807)*
by Joseph Mallord William Turner

NATIONAL GALLERY★★★

***E4** Trafalgar Square -* ⊖ *Charing Cross, Leicester Square, Embankment and Piccadilly Circus -* ☏*020 7747 2885 - www.nationalgallery.org.uk - ♿ - 10h-18h (Fri 21h) - visits and lectures on works of art (from 10 mins to 1hr), Masterpiece Tour (1 hr): see website for programme «tab Visiting» - closed 1ˢᵗ Jan and 24-26 Dec - free (except temporary exhibitions) - audio guide £4 - restaurant, café.*
The nucleus of the collection consisted of 38 pictures amassed by the broker **John Julius Angerstein** (1735-1823) and bought by the government in 1824. To house them, William Wilkins was entrusted with the construction of a museum decorated with a portico of Corinthian columns.

Completed in 1838, it soon proved too small for these ever increasing collections. Alterations and expansions followed until 1991 with the completion of the **Sainsbury Wing**. This is devoted to works prior to 1500 (Italian, Flemish and German schools); Giotto, Leonardo da Vinci and his *Madonna and Child with St. Anne and St. John the Baptist*, a *Battle of San Romano d'Uccello*, Masaccio, Botticelli with *Venus and Mars*, Mantegna, Piero della Francesca with a *Baptism of Christ*, Van Eyck and his *famous Spouses, Arnolfini*, Bosch, Gerard David, Memling, Dürer and the *father of the painter*.

The West Wing is home to 16th century Michelangelo, Titian, Tintoretto alongside Bruegel the Elder, Cranach, Holbein (*The Ambassadors*) and Altdorfer. The Classical period (17th century) is displayed in the **North Wing**. Vermeer (*A Lady Standing at a Virginal*), Ruysdael, Rubens, Rembrandt (*self-portrait aged 34*) and Hals represent the Dutch; Velazquez (*Venus with a Mirror*), Zurbarán, Murillo, for Spain; Italy is present with Caravaggio, Guercino and A. Carrache; Claude Lorrain, Poussin, Philippe de Champaigne with the *portrait of Cardinal de Richelieu* and Le Nain brothers testify to French art. **The East Wing** is dominated by the English from 1700 to 1900 (Constable, Gainsborough, Turner, Reynolds), the Italians (Canaletto, Guardi, Tiepolo), Goya's *Duke of Wellington* and a very rich French 18th century collection; (Chardin, Fragonard , Boucher, Greuze, etc.) and 19th century works; (David, Ingres, Delacroix, Daumier, Courbet, Corot, the Impressionists, Van Gogh's *Sunflowers*, Gauguin, etc.)

NATIONAL PORTRAIT GALLERY★★

E4 St Martin's Place - ⊖ *Leicester Square or Charing Cross - ℘020 7306 0055/12 2463 - www.npg.org.uk - &. - 10h-18h (Thurs - Fri 21h), last admission for exhibits 1 hr before closing - closed 24-26 Dec - free except exhibitions - audio guide £3 - restaurant, café.*

Founded in 1856, then installed in a beautiful Renaissance building behind the National Gallery in 1896 this extraordinary collection brings together more than 12,000 famous British portraits, exhibited in rotation. If certain works were created by the greatest British artists such as Hogarth, Reynolds, Gainsborough or Watts, then the museum is worth a visit for its historical interest. Paintings, drawings, photographs, sculptures and videos reveal the faces of the personalities who forged the history of Britain from the Tudor era to the present day.

The museum is chronologically organized and the visit starts on the 2nd floor with portraits from the Tudor era (16th century) until now.

ST MARTIN-IN-THE FIELDS CHURCH★

E4 Trafalgar Square - ⊖ *Charing Cross - ℘020 7766 1110 - www.stmartin-in-the-fields.org - &. - Mon, Tues and Fri 08h30-13h, 14h-18h; Wed 8h30-13h15, 14h-17h; Thurs 8h30-13h15, 14h-18h , Sat 9h30-18h, Sun 15h30-17h - free guided tour 2 Thursdays a month - audio guide £3.50 - musical schedule (see website).*

Constructed by **James Gibbs** between 1722 and 1726, this church is home to a famous chamber orchestra, decorated with a Corinthian portico and elegant spire. Its crypt houses an amazing café/restaurant (**☝** *p. 114*).

St James's★★

This prestigious area of St James's is home to a royal palace, venerable mansions serving as royal or princely residences, official buildings, gentlemen's clubs and speciality shops and theatres. On the edge of St. James's Park stands Buckingham Palace. The official London residence of the Royal Family, it is accessible to the public in the summer when the Queen goes on holiday. The annexes, the royal stables and the Queen's Gallery stay open all year.

▶**Access:** ⊖ St James's Park, Victoria, Green Park, Charing Cross.
***Map of the area* p. 25. *Detachable map* C/D/E5-6.**
▶**Tip:** Buckingham Palace only opens to the public between Aug and Sept, and Clarence House only in Aug. Tickets are limited so book in advance.

ST JAMES'S PALACE★★

D5 *The palace is closed to the public, except Clarence House in August. Access by Stable Yard -* ⊖ *Green Park -* ☏*030 3123 7324 - www. royalcollection.org.uk - guided tour only (1hr) every 15 mins in Aug: 10h-16h30, w/end 10h-17h30 (last admission 1hr before closing) - £10.*
The Tudor style mansion in which the king and his court settled after the destruction of Whitehall Palace in 1698, was constructed between 1530 and 1532 at the request of Henry VIII. Its crenulated brown brick facade is dominated by an imposing medieval entrance that stands out somewhat next to the Classical architecture of **Pall Mall**★ and St James's Street. Prince Charles lived there until 2004 before moving his sons and Camilla to **Clarence House**, the former residence of the Queen Mother which adjoins the palace.

Distinguished guests stay at **Lancaster House**, a neighbouring mansion used for certain official receptions. In addition, you can access the **Chapel Royal** *(Ambassadors Court - Oct-Jul: Sun 11h15)* and the **Queen's Chapel** *(Marlborough Rd - Oct-Jul: Sun 11h15)*, open only during services. It was here that the coffins of Diana and the Queen Mother were displayed before their funeral.

THE MALL★★

D/E5 ⊖ *Charing Cross.*
It runs along the park to the north and connects Admiralty Arch to **Queen Victoria Memorial** in front of Buckingham Palace. This beautiful tree lined avenue is traversed by the grand royal parades and is dominated by the neoClassical facades of **Carlton House Terrace**, two large residences designed by **John Nash** in 1829.

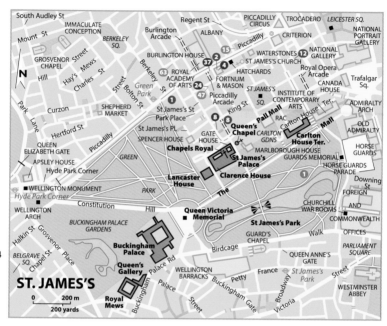

WHERE TO EAT		WHERE TO DRINK		SHOPPING	
Gymkhana	63	Fortnum & Mason's Restaurants	2	Cath Kidston	37
Inn the Park	1	Golden Lion	8	Fortnum & Mason	4
Quaglino's	47	Ole & Steen	12	Hilditch & Key	24
Yoshino	15	Ritz London (The)	1	Lock & Co. Hatters	8

ST JAMES'S PARK★★

D5 🚇 *St James's Park -* 📞*0300 061 2350 - www.royalparks.org.uk - 5h-0h.* This 23 hectare royal park created by Henry VIII in 1532, to brighten up the marshy surroundings of the mansion which had been built (👉 *p. 23*), was redesigned in the 17th century at

Charles II's request, then remodelled in the 19th century by John Nash, George IV's favourite architect. With its floral paths and little lake it is a very pleasant place for walking. The bridge which crosses the lake offers a view of Buckingham Palace and Whitehall.

The Changing of the Guard★★★ at Buckingham Palace

*The Changing of the Guard is one of London's major attractions and usually takes place every other day (consult the calendar on http://changing-guard.com). From 1100, the detachment responsible for Buckingham Palace is inspected, joined 15 mins later by that from St James's Palace. Together they form the «Old guard», as opposed to the «New guard» that will take over. Part of the Wellington Barracks, Regimental Orchestra and Drum Corps arrive at 11:30. It salutes the «Old Guard» before symbolically handing over the Palace keys. Sentinels are then replaced. Thirty five minutes later, the «Old Guard» leaves the Buckingham Palace courtyard to join the Wellington barracks while the «New Guard» splits in two and one detachment heads towards St. James's Palace. The guard is composed of five regiments on foot. They are dressed in a scarlet uniform with dark blue collar and a bearskin cap. They distinguish themselves by the colour of their plume and spacing of buttons; the **Grenadiers** (1656) have a white plume to the left with buttons spaced regularly; the **Coldstream** (1650), a red plume to the right with buttons in pairs and the **Scots** (1642), with no plume and buttons in threes; the **Irish** (1900), a blue plume to the right and buttons in fours; the **Welsh** (1915), a green and white plume on the left and buttons in groups of five.*

25

BUCKINGHAM PALACE★★

D5 *Buckingham Palace Rd -*
⊖ *Victoria -* ☏*020 7766 7324 - www. royalcollection.org.uk -* ♿ *- from end of Jul to end of Aug: 9h30-19h30 (last admission 17h15); Sept: 9h30-18h30 (last admission 16h15) - £23 audio guide included; £39.50 ticket for Queen's Gallery and Royal Mews - online reservation recommended.*
Originally, at this palace that you can admire today, stood a large brick townhouse built in 1702 for the first Duke of Buckingham and acquired in 1762 for the pleasure of **George III**'s young wife, Queen Charlotte. Major changes were made to the building during the next century under the reign of George IV, William IV and Victoria, but the majority of the work was lead by architect John

© Alamy/hemis.fr

St James's Park

Nash. Victoria was the first sovereign to live at Buckingham Palace in 1837 and the Royal Standard has since flown there when the Queen is in residence.

Of the 660 rooms in the palace, only 19, the **State Rooms**, are open to visitors.

These opulent ceremonial rooms are used for receptions and official banquets. The Guard's Hall can be accessed from the Grand Hall and the majestic **Grand Staircase**. You can admire the Green Drawing Room, the State Dining room, the Blue Drawing Room, the Music Room and the White Drawing Room, all lavishly decorated, but the must is to visit the **Throne Room** and **Picture Gallery** where the works of Van Dyck, Rubens, Rembrandt, Vermeer and Canaletto, amongst others, are displayed.

Queen's Gallery★★

By Buckingham Palace Rd - ℰ030 3123 7324 - www.royalcollection. org.uk - ♿ - 10h-17h30 (9h30 from end Jul to Sept, last admission 16h15) - closed from mid Nov to start of Dec and 25-26 Dec - £10.30; ticket includes Royal Mews £17.70, £39.50 including Buckingham Palace and Royal Mews. At the site of an old private chapel, this gallery exhibits portraits, paintings, drawings and furniture in rotation, all from the superb royal collection.

ROYAL MEWS★★

(Royal Stables)
D6 Buckingham Palace Rd - ⊖ Victoria - ℰ030 3123 7324 - www.royalcollection.org.uk - ♿ - Apr-Oct: 10h-17h; Nov & Feb-Mar: every day except Sun:10h-16h (last admission 45 mins before closing) - closed Dec-Jan and official visits - £10 includes audio guide; ticket includes Queen's Gallery £17.70, £39.50 including Queen's Gallery and Buckingham Palace.

A visit to Buckingham Palace would not be complete without visiting the Royal Stables. Here the carriages and official vehicles are kept, used by the Royal Family on their travels. Refurbished by the architect **John Nash**, they were moved here in 1825 under George IV's orders.

The most interesting part of this extraordinary collection of vehicles is the **Golden State Coach** built in 1762 upon George III's request and used for every coronation. Designed by **William Chambers** and made by renowned artists such as the sculptor Joseph Wilton and painter Florentin G. B. Cipriani, it weighs 4 tonnes and needs 8 horses to pull it.

Since the introduction of the first car in King Edward VII's stables, in 1901, the official vehicles are also parked here. The collection comprises 8 limousines: 3 Daimler and 5 Rolls Royce Phantom.

You will also see the immaculate Royal Horse stables for the Windsor Greys and Cleveland Bays, as well as a spectacular saddlery collection.

Mayfair★ and Piccadilly★

Mayfair's name alone is enough to evoke the elegance and luxury symbolized by Bond Street's superb shop windows. To the south, the area is bordered by Piccadilly. Its eastern end, Piccadilly Circus, with its Eros and multitude of luminous signs, is one of the nerve centres of London, and an essential meeting point for all its visitors.

▶**Access:** ⊖ Bond Street, Green Park, Piccadilly Circus, Marble Arch, Hyde Park Corner.
Map of the area p. 28-29. Detachable map C/D4-5.

SHEPHERD MARKET★

*C5 ⊖ Green Park -
www.shepherdmarket.co.uk.*
This **market** consists of a maze of alleys and paved courtyards connected by arched passages. The Victorian and Edwardian pubs, the little houses with stalls on the ground floor, outdoor foreign restaurants and an **antique market** give the place a cosmopolitan village atmosphere.

BERKELEY SQUARE

C4 ⊖ Green Park.
The memory of Berkeley wood lives on thanks to plane trees planted in 1789. The square was remodelled in 1737. On the west side, some 18th century houses with their wrought iron balconies, door lanterns and link extinguishers remain from the former architectural style.

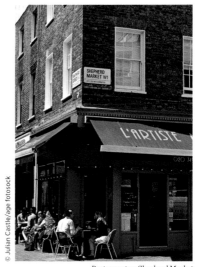

© Julian Castle/age fotosock

Restaurant on Shepherd Market

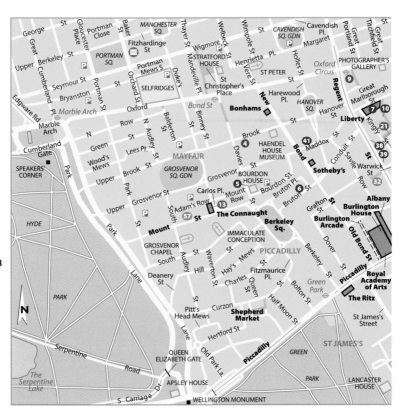

MOUNT STREET

C4 ⊖ *Marble Arch or Hyde Park Corner.*

An atmosphere of tranquillity reigns in Mount Street which ends up at the northwest corner of Berkeley Square and passes in front of **the Connaught**, a building iconic of luxury hotels, from the end of the 19th century. Lined with tall brick houses, with irregular terracotta adorned gables, this street offers passers-by numerous shop windows; antique furniture, paintings, porcelain etc. During the Civil War, members of Parliament raised barricades here, explaining the name and topography of the place.

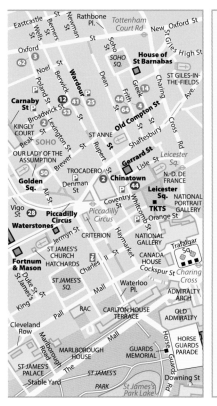

29

BOND STREET★

C/D4 ⊖ *Bond Street.*

This old Tudor lane crosses Mayfair from north to south. **New Bond Street**, built in 1720, included high society amongst its residents, who used the bespoke tailors and perfumers of the area. Since then it has become THE most elegant street, lined with luxury leather goods, fashion designers, chic stationers and art dealers. **Sotheby's** at No. 35 has become the world's largest auction house since its beginnings in 1744. Its largest rival, **Bonham's** is located in the same area *(7 Blenheim St.)*. **Old Bond Street★** extends past the bronze sculpture paying homage to Churchill and Roosevelt and is lined with well-respected luxury businesses (porcelain, jewellery, antiques, etc.). **Burlington Arcade**'s regency passage is close by.

BURLINGTON HOUSE★

D4 ⊖ *Piccadilly Circus.*
In 1664 the 1st Earl of Burlington acquired this property. His descendant began to reconstruct it in 1715 in the Palladian style. Restored in the 19th century, the building was modified again in neo-Renaissance style between 1867-1873. In 1869, the back of Burlington House was transformed in neo-Gothic style. Decorated with towers, a portico and huge porch, this wing of the building displays 20 statues of magistrates. **The Royal Academy of Art**'s headquarters are based here which supports the contemporary creation and organizes numerous exhibitions. (*☏020 7300 8090 - www. royalacademy.org.uk - ♿ - 10h-18h [Fri 22h], last admission 30 mins before closing - prices according to exhibitions, free guided tour of permanent collections: see website for calendar).*

PICCADILLY★

C/D4-5 ⊖ *Piccadilly Circus or Hyde Park Corner.*
This famous London artery stretches from Piccadilly Circus to Hyde Park Corner, separating St. James's (♿ *p. 23*) and Mayfair's neighbourhoods. It is lined with elegant buildings, exclusive clubs, luxurious shops and prestigious hotels like **The Ritz.** Since its opening in 1906, this classic French inspired hotel, decorated in Louis XVI style, welcomes V.I.P.S.

Fortnum & Mason
181 Piccadilly.
Founded in 1707, this internationally acclaimed delicatessen is also famous for its musical clock which sounds every hour and represents the two founders of the store.
♿ *Addresses /Shopping p. 132.*

PICCADILLY CIRCUS★

D4 ⊖ *Piccadilly Circus.*
Formerly considered the centre of the British Empire, this noisy crossroad meets three major roads. Its beautiful **fountain** was built in 1893 in homage to Lord Shaftesbury (1801-1885), the famous British philanthropist. On top of it, the bronze *Angel of Christian Charity* commonly mistaken for Eros has become one of the capital's icons, as have the neon signs here.

Piccadilly Circus.

Soho★

This bohemian area sometimes has a gloomy atmosphere.
Soho is frequented by advertisers, the film and fashion industries, and is also home to the gay community. In the evening, night owls frequent the pubs and French, Italian, Greek, Chinese and West Indian restaurants, while the crowd flocks around the theatres, cinemas, jazz clubs and nightclubs.

▶**Access:** ⊖ Oxford Circus, Tottenham Court Road, Leicester Square, Piccadilly Circus.
***Map of the area** p. 28-29.* ***Detachable map** D/E3-4.*

REGENT STREET★★

D4 ⊖ *Oxford Circus or Piccadilly Circus.*
Although the historic Dickins and Jones department store closed its doors in 2007, this major and elegant street built under the direction of John Nash, remains a shopping mecca. Among others you can find Hamley's enormous toy shop, Austin Reed, Hunter, Jaeger, Tommy Hilfiger, Anthropologie, etc., without forgetting the famous Café Royal.

LIBERTY★★

D4 *Great Marlborough St.-*
⊖ *Oxford Circus.*
The shop was founded in 1875 by Arthur Liberty and was originally located on Regent Street itself. You can find a vast choice of imported items from the British Empire in this «Emporium», supplemented by furniture made in Soho's workshops. The shop has created its own product lines, copies of traditional Indian designs or commissioned by leading creators of aesthetics and the Arts and Crafts movement. Art Nouveau designed jewellery is imported from the continent, but the Liberty brand is especially famous for its fine and delicate cotton fabrics with very characteristic floral patterns, popularized in France by Cacharel in the 1960s.

Note the magnificent colonnaded facade on Regent Street, dominated by the monumental statue of *Britannia* surrounded by three stone figures.
The Tudor **facade** (1924) on Great Marlborough Street (the shop's main entrance) was designed by Edwin T. and Stanley Hall, constructed using oak and teak from the last two schooners belonging to the Royal Navy. ♿*Addresses / Shopping p. 132.*

CARNABY STREET

D4 ⊖ *Oxford Circus.*
This mainly pedestrianized area around **Carnaby Street** (Foubert's Place, Kingly Street, Beak Street, etc.), was a hotspot for Swinging London in the 1960s, before taking on an

32

Chinatown with the new year decorations

extremely commercial character. It has changed again and is now home to sophisticated shops, trendy bars, restaurants and clubs. Explore the alleys and courtyards around, such as the pretty **Kingly Court**, whose passages are home to cafés and restaurants.

GOLDEN SQUARE

D4 ⊖ *Piccadilly Circus.*
This beautiful square which has a garden enclosed by railings, is the preserve of the fashion and media world. Calm prevails in contrast to the hustle and bustle of the area.

WARDOUR STREET

D3-4 ⊖ *Leicester Square.*
A symbol of the 1930's film industry, the street has remained home to many film production houses. At night activities are in full swing. There's a succession of bars and restaurants.

HOUSE OF ST BARNABAS

D3 1 Greek Street - ⊖ *Tottenham Court Road - www.hosb.org.uk - Do not visit.*
This house, built around 1750, is a very active association today reintegrating the homeless. The entrance is flanked by two obelisks while the inner rooms are decorated with stuccoes. There's a surprising little neo-Gothic chapel designed in 1863.

OLD COMPTON STREET

D4 ⊖ *Piccadilly Circus.*
Lined with pubs, restaurants, wine merchants, pastry shops and Italian delicatessens, this road is one of the meeting places for the gay community.

CHINATOWN★

D4 ⊖ *Leicester Square.*
Guarded by large oriental porticoes, Gerrard Street is the centre of this colourful area, striking due to the exotic character of its restaurants, shops and other centres of Chinese medicine. This is where the traditional Chinese New Year celebrations are held (*Jan or Feb*).

LEICESTER SQUARE★

D/E4 ⊖ *Leicester Square.*
Recently renovated and entirely pedestrianized, this vast square has been the heart of London's show business, as witnessed by the Empire Theatre building (1884) to the north of the square. Today, lined with shops, restaurants and cinemas, Leicester Square is an animated and popular place to go, where you can enjoy a break opposite the fountain built in Shakespeare's memory in 1874.
On the south side, the **TKTS kiosk** sells half price theatre tickets for the same day.

Covent Garden★

Covent Garden is not the most typical area of London, but it is the beating heart of the tourist centre. Onlookers who come to stroll along the Piazza replace the traders who once encroached the edge of the market. In the evening, pub goers spill onto the pavements, and theatregoers flock to the restaurants before attending one of the many shows in the area.

▶**Access:** ⊖ Covent Garden.
Map of the area p. 36. Detachable map E4.

THE PIAZZA★

E4 Built on the site of a convent's garden (*convent;* in fact Westminster Abbey), this place was conceived by **Inigo Jones** in 1631 at the demand of Francis Russell, 4th Earl of Bedford who became the owner of the estate after the Reform. The famous architect (♿ *p. 168*) was inspired by the Place Royale, Paris (now Place des Vosges) and the Piazza Grande di Livorno (Italy) which he had admired several years beforehand. From the square that Inigo Jones conceived nothing remains except the houses to the west of Russell Street (reconstructed).

COVENT GARDEN MARKET

E4 In the beautiful hall, the former flower, fruit and vegetable market founded in the 16th century (and made famous by G. B. Shaw's Eliza Doolittle), was transferred to Nine Elms (next to Vauxhall) in 1974 and replaced by a craft market.
Shops, cafés and restaurants were relocated to the former warehouses,

© Ben Pipe/www.visitlondon.com

Covent Garden Market decorated for Christmas

designed by Charles Fowler in 1832 and connected by glass roofs in 1872.

ROYAL OPERA HOUSE★

E4 Bow St. - ☎020 7304 4000 - www.roh.org.uk - guided tour of the theatre (1hr15) and auditorium (45

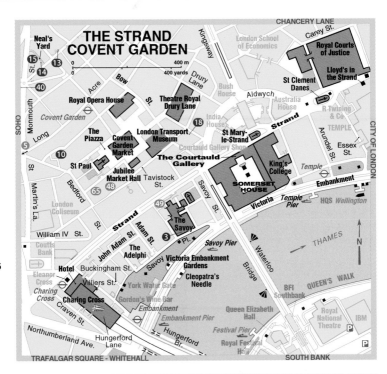

THE STRAND COVENT GARDEN

WHERE TO EAT		WHERE TO DRINK		SHOPPING	
Abeno Too	5	Lamb & Flag	10	Magma	13
Flat Iron	65	Primrose Bakery	18	Neal's Yard Dairy	14
Rules	48	Savoy (The)	3	Neal's Yard Remedies	15
Simpson's-in-the-Strand	49			Tatty Devine	40

36

mins), on reservation, see calendar on website - £12/£ 9.50 (children less than 8 years not admitted).
The **Royal Opera** was founded in 1732. The present building, built between 1856 and 1858 by Edward M. Barry, is the third theatre to be built on this site and underwent major renovations in the 1990s. Dedicated to opera and ballet, its hall has a seating capacity of more than 2,200 and hosts the Royal Opera, the Royal Ballet and the Royal Orchestra.

THEATRE ROYAL DRURY LANE

E4 Founded in 1663, it is the fourth theatre built on the site of the earliest building built in the Restoration. The current building is the work of Benjamin Wyatt. It was there in 1665 that King Charles II met the English actress Nell Gwyn (1650-1687), the most famous of his mistresses, and with whom he had two illegitimate children.

LONDON TRANSPORT MUSEUM★

E4 *Covent Garden Piazza - ☏020 7379 6344 - www.ltmuseum.co.uk - ♿ - Sun-Thurs 10h-18h, Fri 11h-18h (last admission 17h15) - £17.50 (ticket valid for a year) - Under 18s free.*
Very popular with families, this interactive museum revisits 200 years of history and technology. Established in 1920 and 1930 by the London General Omnibus Company, the collection was transferred to this former flower market in 1980. The exhibitions include audio visual animations and show the development and impact of its urban transport networks on London, one of the largest in the world. You can also see vehicles such as Shillibeer's horse drawn omnibus (1829-1834), an Underground train motor from 1866 or the first bus from 1910.

NEAL'S YARD★

E4 *Between Shorts Garden and Monmouth St.*
Vegetarian restaurants, cheese, organic and alternative medicine shops have come to settle in this picturesque and vibrant courtyard, which has retained its old world charm with its lifting systems, dovecotes, window boxes and decorative trees in tubs.

JUBILEE MARKET HALL

E4 Souvenir vendors occupy the hall from Tuesday to Friday, followed by arts and crafts on Saturdays and Sundays, and antique dealers on Mondays. Jubilee Hall (1904) is home to a gym.

ST PAUL'S CHURCH★

E4 *Entrance on Bedford St. - ☏020 7836 5221 - www.actorschurch.org - ♿ - Mon-Fri 8h30-17h, Sun 9h-13h, Sat: check website.*
This harmonious Tuscan style pink brick church, built by Jones in 1633, was faithfully rebuilt after the fire that damaged it in 1795. It is also known as *the Actors' Church*, because its vaults and cemetery are home to several celebrities, including the sculptor **Grinling Gibbons**.

Strand ★

Located on the edge of Covent Garden and the City, the area has many assets, despite the constant flow of traffic. Lined with beautiful buildings inherited from its aristocratic past, it is home to elegant hotels, theatres and, beautiful art collections at Somerset House, whilst remaining true to its reputation as an area to go out in.

▶ **Access:** ⊖ Temple, Charing Cross, Embankment.
Map of the area p. 36. ***Detachable map*** E/F4-5.

CHARING CROSS STATION

E4-5 ⊖ *Charing Cross or Embankment.*
Serving the south of England (like Victoria station), Charing Cross station was built in 1863. Just next door, the neo-Gothic **Charing Cross Hotel** (1864)(now an Amba hotel) whose two upper floors were added later, is the work of E. M. Barry. To the rear, the buildings conceived by Terry Farrell (1990) are impressive due to a great white arch, that partially covers the railway viaduct.
A collectors market (**Charing Cross Collectors Market**) is held on Saturdays at the end of Villiers Street, under the viaduct.

VICTORIA EMBANKMENT GARDENS★

E4 ⊖ *Embankment.*
In **Victoria Wharf**, the gardens were created in 1864, concerts are held there in the summer. On the other side, by the edge of the river, stands **Cleopatra's Needle**, an Egyptian pink granite obelisk erected in 1878 and donated to George IV by Muhammad Ali. This is not the original needle, which is now found in Central Park, New York. Without its pedestal, the obelisk measures 21m in height (the one in New York: 23.5m, the one in Rome: 25m) and weighs 182.5t.

THE ADELPHI

E4 ⊖ *Charing Cross or Embankment.*
This sheltered area is wedged between the Strand and the Thames, from Villiers Street to Adam Street. In the 18th and 19th centuries it was a sort of little Athens favoured by artists. From 1768, the three **Adam brothers** (architects), built the Adelphi area. They created an urban development following a regular design whose streets were lined with similar, antique style facades. Unfortunately, the Adam family went broke and the houses almost all disappeared from the second half of the 19th century. At least two beautiful examples survive, typical of the Adam style. At No. 8 **John Adam Street**, the charming black facade, of the **Royal Society of**

Ice-skating rink, Somerset House

39

Arts (1774) surmounted by a beautiful statue, visible from the top of the staircase that connects Durham House Street to the Strand. A little further on, at No. 7 Adam Street, a house features pilasters with honeysuckle carvings.

THE SAVOY★

E4 ⊖ *Charing Cross.*
The Savoy is a complex comprising a chapel, a theatre built by Richard d'Oyly Carte in 1881, the first electrically lit London building, and an exceptional hotel by the same architect. Typically British, the Savoy **Hotel**, one of London's most famous, occupies the site of the Savoy palace built in 1246 by Henry III Plantagenet and residence of Peter II, Count of Savoy. It reopened in 2010 after major renovation works that required the work of 1,000 workers, artists and craftsmen!

SOMERSET HOUSE★★

E4 Access from Strand and Victoria Embankment - ⊖ *Temple - ✆020 7845 4600 - www.somersethouse. org.uk - free guided tour (45 mins-1hr): Tues 12h45 and 14h15, Thurs 13h15 and 14h45, Sat every hour between 12h15 and 15h15.*
This beautiful Portland stone building stretching between the Strand and

the Thames was designed by architect **William Chambers** (♿ *p. 169*) and built at the end of the 18th century, on the site of an old royal palace wanted by Lord Protector and Duke of Somerset in 1547. Its narrow facade on the Strand is not very impressive, but you can see the beauty of the place on the other side of the portico. A vast courtyard is spiked by elegant jets of water which bring happiness to both young and old in the summer. Many activities (concerts, sound and light shows, etc.) are organized on Somerset House's piazza throughout the year.

THE COURTAULD GALLERY ★★

E4 *Somerset House* - ⊖ *Temple* - *☎020 7848 2526 - http://courtauld. ac.uk -* ♿ *- 10h-18h (last admission 17h30) - closed 25-26 Dec - £7.*
Known under the name of **Fine Rooms**, these showrooms providing access to the Strand, with exceptional proportions and elegant stucco ceilings, house the Courtauld Institute of art's collections, bequeathed to the University of London; the exceptional collection of Samuel Courtauld's **impressionist** works comprising the canvases of Manet (*A Bar at the Folies-Bergère*), Van Gogh (*Self-Portrait with Bandaged Ear*), Cézanne (*Lake Annecy*), etc.; Princes Gate Collection comprising 30 of **Rubens**' oil paintings and 6 drawings by **Michel-Ange** as well as paintings by Bruegel, Leonardo da Vinci, Tiepolo, Dürer, Rembrandt, Bellini, Tintoret and Kokoschka. You will also see early paintings by Italian Renaissance artists, as well as paintings from the **Bloomsbury Group**.
The collection, displayed on rotation, is enriched by the long-term loan of masterpieces from the 19th and 20th centuries, including private collections; paintings (Matisse, Derain, Dufy, Léger, Delaunay, Kandinsky) and sculptures (Degas, Rodin, Moore, Hepworth).

ST MARY-LE-STRAND

E4 *The Strand* - ⊖ *Temple* - *☎020 7836 3126 - www.stmarylestrand.org - Tues-Fri 11h-16h, Sun 10h-13h.*
Built by **James Gibbs** between 1714 and 1724, this baroque style church has a semi-circular porch, a flat roof and storeyed steeple topped with a lantern. Inside, its coffered ceiling is carved with floral motifs or cherubs. Apart from the steeple, the building looks like a small palace.
St Mary-le-Strand known as one of the «Island Churches».

ST CLEMENT DANES ★

F4 *St Clement Danes Church Strand* - ⊖ *Temple* - *☎020 7242 8282 - www. raf.mod.uk/stclementdanes -* ♿ *9h-16h, Sat 10h-15h, Sun 9h30-15h - closed during public holidays.*
Danes were formerly buried in this place where **Wren** built the current building and steeple in 1682, rebuilt by **Gibbs** in 1719. It presents a certain number of similarities with that of St. Mary. The church, burnt in 1941, was restored between 1955 and 1958 under the auspices of the Royal Air Force which became the

© ultraforma/iStockphoto.com

The Strand, St Mary-the-Strand in the background

sanctuary (735 badges are buried in the ground). The very harmonious interior, has benches and rostrums dear to **Wren**; their dark hues contrast with the light tones of the pillars and the white stuccoed vault stands against the grey background. Pulpit by **Grinling Gibbons**.

ROYAL COURTS OF JUSTICE

F4 ⊖ *Temple.* **The Palace of Justice** is an important building of Perpendicular style, built between 1874 and 1882. The judges sit in scarlet robes with a livery collar and long wig, while the lawyers wear a gown and short wig.

LLOYD'S IN THE STRAND

F4 222 Strand - ⊖ *Temple.*
The **Palsgrave Head Tavern** owes its name to Count Palsgrave Frederick, who married James I's daughter Elizabeth and later became King of Bohemia. The memory of these three people is recalled in the unusual Doulton earthenware depiction of this building which served as a courthouse restaurant from 1883. Since 1895, the building housed a Lloyds bank branch until the 14th of August 2017 when it closed.

Temple★ and Fleet Street

Temple and Fleet Street refer to two different traditions; English law for the former and publishing for the latter.

▶ **Access:** ⊖ Temple.
Map of the area see opposite. Detachable map F4.

TEMPLE★

F4 *Access from Inner Temple Gateway (between Nos. 16 and 17 Fleet St.).*
A surprising maze of courtyards, arches, passages and gardens going down to the banks of the Thames. These lands owe their name to the Knights Templar established here in the 12 century, before giving way to The Order of Malta, and were occupied by schools and law firms. Today, dedicated to legal activities, it's a true haven of peace, home to 17th and 18th century buildings.

Temple Church★★

King's Bench Walk - ☎020 7353 8559 - www.templechurch.com - ♿ - Mon-Fri 10h-16h, but with exceptions - consult the online calendar - £5.
Built in the 12th century to a circular design characteristic of churches belonging to The Order of Malta, it has a Roman porch.

FLEET STREET

F4 It was the area of choice for journalists until technology transformed the production of major newspapers, and they moved their offices to Docklands. This major artery, which is also a royal road, is lined with impressive buildings of very different styles. At No. 1, Child and Co. (a subsidiary of the Royal Bank of Scotland) has pride of place as the oldest English bank.

ST BRIDE'S★

F4 Fleet St. - ⊖ Blackfriars - ☎020 7427 0133 - www.stbrides.com - Mon-Fri 8h-18h, Sat variable opening hrs, Sun 10h-18h30, closed public holidays - guided tour Tue 15h (except Dec) - £6 - free concerts (see schedule online).
Wren's famous St. Bride's church and **white spire★★** were burnt down in 1940. Only the shell and bell tower remained. The exterior of the building was restored to Wren's original design, with large curved windows between pedimented semi circular headed doors. Inside, a neo-Classical altar closes the nave and apse.

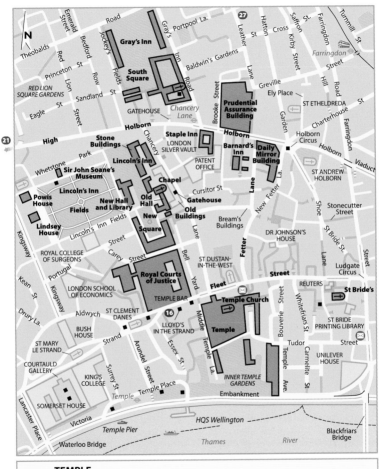

N

Theobalds Road
Emerald Street
Jockey's Fields
Gray's Inn Road
Portpool La.
Leather St
Hatton
Cross
Saffron St.
Farringdon
Turnmill St.

Bedford Row
Red Lion St
Princeton St
Sandland St
Eagle St
RED LION SQUARE GARDENS

Gray's Inn
South Square
Baldwin's Gardens
Greville St
Ely Place
Farringdon

GATEHOUSE
Chancery Lane
Prudential Assurance Building
ST ETHELDREDA

Kirby Street
Hatton Garden

21 🚇
High Holborn
Whetstone Park
Stone Buildings
Staple Inn
LONDON SILVER VAULT
Holborn
Barnard's Inn
Daily Mirror Building
Holborn Circus
Charterhouse St
Holborn Viaduct
ST ANDREW HOLBORN

Lincoln's Inn
PATENT OFFICE
Leather Lane
New Fetter Lane
Shoe Lane
Stonecutter Street

Sir John Soane's Museum
Chapel
Cursitor St
Gatehouse
Old Hall
Old Buildings
Bream's Buildings
DR JOHNSON'S HOUSE
St Bride St
43

Powis House
Lincoln's Inn Fields
New Hall and Library
New Square
Lindsey House
Lincoln's Inn Fields

ROYAL COLLEGE OF SURGEONS
Carey Street
Portugal St
LONDON SCHOOL OF ECONOMICS
Bell Yard
ST DUSTAN-IN-THE-WEST
Fetter Street
Ludgate Circus

Kingsway
Kean St
Drury La.
Royal Courts of Justice
TEMPLE BAR
ST CLEMENT DANES
Fleet Street
REUTERS
St Bride's

ST MARY LE STRAND
BUSH HOUSE
16
LLOYD'S IN THE STRAND
Temple Church
Temple
Bouverie Street
Whitefriars St
ST BRIDE PRINTING LIBRARY

Aldwych
Strand
Arundel Street
Essex St
Middle Temple La.
Temple La.
Tudor St
Carmelite St
UNILEVER HOUSE

COURTAULD GALLERY
KING'S COLLEGE
SOMERSET HOUSE
Surrey St
Temple Place
Temple
INNER TEMPLE GARDENS
Temple Ave.
Street

Lancaster Place
Victoria Embankment
Temple Pier
HQS Wellington
Thames River
Blackfriars Bridge
Waterloo Bridge

**TEMPLE
FLEET STREET
CHANCERY LANE**

0 _____ 200 m
   200 yards

WHERE TO DRINK

Craft Beer Co..............................**27**

Princess Louise...........................**21**

SHOPPING

Twinings......................................**16**

Chancery Lane★

Defined by High Holborn and Fleet Street, this area owes its character to the ancient traditions of the Inns of Court. Take time to stroll through the alleyways to discover the fascinating history and continuity through the ages, hidden behind the current sites. The green and peaceful squares allow you to escape the crowds of visitors and customers from the shopping centres.

▶**Access:** ⊖ Holborn, Chancery Lane.
Map of the area *p. 43.* **Detachable map** *E/F3.*

LINCOLN'S INN FIELDS

E3 ⊖ *Holborn.* By 1650, a developer, who had acquired the grounds extending to the west of Lincoln's Inn, built houses on three sides of the garden, a haven of peace in the heart of a very busy area. One of them, **Lindsey House**, probably designed by Inigo Jones, still exists, although divided in two today (Nos. 59 and 60). Several houses date from the 18th century, such as Nos. 57 and 58, built in 1730 in the Palladian style, and **Powis House** (1777) at No. 66, whose main bay window is finished with a pediment. On the north side, Nos. 1-2 are from the start of the 18th century, Nos. 5 to 9 are Georgian and No. 15 is from the middle of the 18th century. To the south side rise official buildings; the Jacobean style building formerly occupied until 2010 by the **Land Registry**, the Neo-Georgian Nuffield College of Surgical Science (1956-1958) and the Royal College of Surgeons (late 19th-early 20th century). At the corner of Portsmouth Street, a partially timbered building displays the date 1567.

SIR JOHN SOANE'S MUSEUM★★

E3 13 Lincoln's Inn Fields - ⊖ *Holborn -* 📞*020 7405 2107 - www.soane.org -* ♿ *Tues-Sat 10h-17h (last admission 30 mins before closing), candlelight tours every 1st Tues of the month 18h-21h - free - audio guide - guided tour Tues and Sat 11h and 12h, Thurs - Fri 12h, £10 - closed on public holidays.*

Between 1792 and 1823, the **architect John Soane** acquired, remodelled and constructed Nos. 12, 13 and 14 Lincoln's Inn Fields as his family home, offices and a museum. In 1833, the British Parliament voted for a resolution guaranteeing the sustainability of his museum after his death, without any modification to the interior. The collections, besides their own interest, allow you to enter into the universe of a great collector from this era to experience its unusual charm.

The rooms are small, the corridors narrow, the stairs modest, but the ingenious arrangement of mirrors, movable partitions, lighting and

44

Inns of Court

The Inns of courts, the capital's law schools, oversee the profession and prepare students who have completed their law studies for bar admission.
*Gray's Inn, Lincoln Inn, Inner Temple and Middle Temple together form **Chancery Lane**, the backbone of legal London. The buildings cannot be visited, but during the day, on weekdays, it is pleasant to mix with the flow of lawyers rushing to get to their studies, to stroll along the shady paths that border the gardens or among the labyrinth of courtyards and tall 15th and 18th century buildings.*

windows onto courtyards and decor increase the volume, surfaces and perspectives.

Fragments, casts and models are exhibited on both sides of the galleries, while in the basement is the crypt (urns and funeral vases), the monk's parlour and the sepulchral chamber containing the sarcophagus of Seti (around 1300 BC.).

On the first floor models, prints, architectural plans and rare books are displayed. The south living room contains a picture by Turner, hung in front of the fireplace.

On the ground floor are the dining room, the office, the dome shaped breakfast room and Lawrence's very evocative 75-year-old portrait of Soane. The **collection of paintings** (picture gallery) includes original drawings by Piranesi, **Hogarth's** satirical scenes, but also paintings by Canaletto, Reynolds and Turner. In the basement, the old kitchens contain the oldest patented stove in the world.

LINCOLN'S INN ★★

F3 ⊖ *Chancery Lane - ☏020 7405 1393 - www.lincolnsinn.org.uk - park: Mon-Fri 7h-19h - chapel: Mon-Fri 9h-17h - closed on public holidays. No guided tours until Jan 2018 due to renovation work.*

The site belonged to the Dominicans until 1276 and was then acquired by the Earl of Lincoln who built a large house that became a residence for law students. A main gate gives access to the entanglement of courtyards and buildings surrounded by gardens and sheds. Constructions from the 17th century, occupied mainly by law students, surround **New Square**. The Classical style **Stone Buildings** were built around 1775. **The New Hall** and **Library** occupy a large Tudor style building (1845-73). The southern part is marked by gabled Tudor style brick buildings (rebuilt in 1609); **Old Buildings**. The oldest building in Lincoln's Inn, the **Old Hall**, dates from 1490. **The chapel** (accessed by stairs to the left of the Old Hall), Gothic in style, was rebuilt between 1619 and 1623. The windows from the same period are by Flemish artists, the Van Linge brothers.

Lawyers would formerly receive their customers in the low gallery. The names and coats of arms of the faithful and Treasurers have been added to the Gatehouse; Thomas More, Richard Cromwell, Horace Walpole, William Pitt, Lord Brougham, Disraeli, etc. **The Gatehouse**, made of brick and corner turrets, dates from 1518. The massive oak doors that close the four arches are original. The arms of Henry VIII, the Earl of Lincoln and Sir Thomas Lovell appear just above.

GRAY'S INN ★

E/F3 South Square - ⊖ *Chancery Lane.*

The foundations of this law school go back to the 14th century, whereas the buildings date back to the 16th century. The main entrance is marked by an elegant guardroom dated 1688. Inside the surrounding enclosure, **South Square**, completely reconstructed with the exception of No.1 which dates back to 1685, is decorated with a beautiful bronze statue of the philosopher **Francis Bacon**, Gray Inn's most illustrious member. The hall was rebuilt in the style of the 16th century with crow stepped gables and a late Perpendicular tracery. The gardens were then one of Londoners' favourite walks, enclosed to the south by magnificent wrought iron railings from the beginning of the 18th century.

STAPLE INN ★

F3 ⊖ *Chancery Lane.*

At the edge of the City, Staple Inn is one of nine Inns of Chancery originally attached to Gray's Inn where law students spent their first year. Partly built of wood, it is one of the very few examples of medieval London.

The facade on Holborn, with corbelled sides and balconies, dates between 1586 and 1596 and is the only surviving example of Elizabethan urban architecture in the city. A vaulted passage provides access to a charming courtyard surrounded by 18th century buildings, beyond which extends a garden.

HIGH HOLBORN

F3 ⊖ *Chancery Lane.*

On the way to Holborn Circus stands the massive red **Prudential Insurance Building**, designed by A. Waterhouse (early 20th century). Just opposite, **Barnard's Inn** is now home to **Gresham College**, London's first free university. Founded in 1597 by Sir Thomas Gresham in his Bishopsgate residence in the heart of the City, the institution moved into these buildings in 1843. On the same side of the street, between Fetter Lane and New Fetter Lane, the curious **Daily Mirror Building** distinguished by its stone facade, was 50m high and supported and dominated by glass buildings (1957-1960).

The City★★★
(The Square Mile)

Also known as the «Square Mile», the City extends over the north bank of the Thames. It is limited by the route of the old London wall which defined the Roman and medieval city. Under the effect of its extraordinary success, a financial district of the capital, world market and place of prime importance, the City has metamorphosed and has many great architectural achievements. Mainly a place of work, it is nevertheless dotted with bars, restaurants and shops.

▶**Access:** ⊖ St Paul's, Mansion House, Bank, Cannon Street, Monument, Aldgate, Barbican, Liverpool Street.
***Map of the area** p. 50-51. **Detachable map** F/G/H3-4.*
▶**Tip:** visit the City on a weekday because at the weekend and in the evening the area is deserted.

ST PAUL'S CATHEDRAL★★★

48

G4 St Paul's Churchyard - ⊖ St Paul's - ℘020 7246 8350 - www.stpauls.co.uk - ♿ - Mon-Sat 8h30-16h30, galleries: 9h30-16h15 - guided tour (around 1hr 30): at 10h, 11h, 13h and 14h - £18 including audio guide.
Crowning the City with its gigantic dome, St. Paul's Cathedral, a masterpiece by **Christopher Wren** (♿ p. 169), stands on **Ludgate Hill**. The first stone of the cathedral, designed by Wren after the Great Fire, was laid on June 21, 1675. Thirty-three years later, the architect was able to see his son placing the last stone of the building at the top of the lantern.

Exterior
It is from the esplanade to the south of the monument that the most spectacular perspective can be found. Unlike St. Peter's dome, which influenced Wren, **St. Paul's dome★★★** does not really have the shape of a hemisphere. Its drum is on two levels; the lower level is surrounded by a colonnade and capped with a balustrade, while the upper level forms a circular panoramic gallery, the **Stone Gallery**. At the top of the dome, the lantern is in sober English Baroque style, with columns on all four sides and a small cupola serving as a plinth for the golden ball, 2m in diameter.
The **west extremity**, preceded by two broad flights of stairs, has a portico with two levels and columns under a decorated pediment, topped by the portrait of Saint Paul. On the other side all the way up are the most Baroque towers ever made by **Wren** so as to highlight the dome. Do not miss out on the outdoor sculptures, made in part by **Grinling Gibbons**.

© High Level Photograph/Loop Images/age fotostock

St Paul's Cathedral

Interior

Rich and impressive, it is worth seeing for the breath-taking presence of its big dome, as wide as the nave and aisles together, and decorated by **James Thornhill**'s faded paintings. In the nave, notice Wellington's imposing mausoleum, opposite, in the north transept hangs *The Light of the World*, a painting created in 1900 by W. Holman Hunt. From the **Whispering Gallery** located under the dome (259 steps), the visitor will be impressed by the breath-taking views of the transept and dome. Note the strange sound effect that earned the gallery its name. **The panoramic view★★★** from the **Golden Gallery**, at the top of the dome (543 steps), allows you to discover London and the Thames.

The arms of the transept are not very wide. The left arm contains baptismal fonts carved in 1727 by **Francis Bird**; the right houses the magnificent statue of Nelson by **Flaxman**. In the choir, the magnificent **stalls★★** are the work of Gibbons. The graceful sculpture of the Madonna and Child by **Henry Moore** (1984) in the northeast aisle. In the right hand ambulatory, note the astonishing statue of the poet John Donne, Dean of St Paul between 1621 and 1631, as well as Bill Viola's curious video installations.

Clerkenwell Rd
Turnmill St
Britton St
John's La.
John St
A1
Golden La.
Fortune St
Whitecross St
Lamb's Passage
Bunhill Row
City Rd
Tabernacle St
Finsbury Square

Farringdon
Benjamin St
Cowcross St
A201
Charterhouse
CHARTERHOUSE SQ.
Chiswell St
Milton St
Ropemaker St
Finsbury Square
Lackington St

SMITHFIELD MARKET
Charterhouse
Long La.
Barbican
Aldersgate St
Barbican Arts Centre
Silk St
Moor La.
Moorgate
Moorgate

W Smithfield
St Bartholomew-the-Great
ST GILES CRIPPLEGATE
Fore St
Finsbury Circus

Hosier La.
Cock La.
ST BARTHOLOMEW'S HOSPITAL
Museum of London
London Wall
BARBICAN
Basinghall St
Wall
Copthall Ave.

Snow Hill
Newgate St
King Edward St
St Martin's le Grand
Noble St
Wood St
Love La.
Throgmorton Ave.

City Thameslink
Fleet Passage
Gresham St
Gutter La.
Foster La.
Guildhall
Coleman St
Moorgate
St Margaret Lothbury

Bride St
Limeburner La.
Old Bailey
St Paul's
Guildhall Art Gallery & London's Roman Amphitheatre
ST VEDAST
Museum
Bank of England
Royal Exchange

Ludgate Hill
ST BRIDE'S
ST PAUL'S CATHEDRAL
St Paul's Churchyard
Cheapside
St Mary-le-Bow
Watling St
ST MARY ALDERMARY
Mansion House
ST MICHAEL'S
Cornhill
King William St
ST MARY WOOLNOTH

Tudor St
Carmelite St
Blackfriars
Carter La.
Knightrider St
Queen Victoria St
COLE ABBEY PRESBYTERIAN
Mansion House
Cannon
Cloak La.
College St
St Stephen Walbrook
Walbrook
ST MICHAEL'S
St Swithin's La.
Cannon Street

Blackfriars Bridge
Millennium Bridge
Upper ST. JAMES GARLICKHYTHE
Tallow Chandler's Hall
Skinner's Hall
Street
Cannon Street
Monument
The Monument

Upper Ground
Rennie St
Paris Garden
A201
BANKSIDE GALLERY
TATE MODERN
Hopton St
Holland St
Bankside
SHAKESPEARE'S GLOBE
ROSE THEATRE
Sumner St
Park St
Southwark Bridge
Great Guildford St
Southwark Bridge Rd
Cousin La.
Thames St
Angel La.
Swan La.
CANNON STREET
London Bridge
SOUTHWARK CATHEDRAL
Duke St Hill
BOROUGH

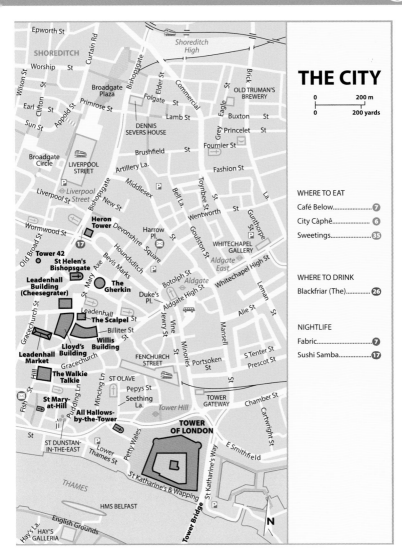

THE CITY

```
0              200 m
0              200 yards
```

WHERE TO EAT

Café Below.......................7
City Càphê........................6
Sweetings......................35

WHERE TO DRINK

Blackfriar (The)...............26

NIGHTLIFE

Fabric............................7
Sushi Samba...................17

51

Map labels:

Epworth St
SHOREDITCH
Worship St
Wilson St
Curtain Rd
Shoreditch High
Broadgate Plaza
Bishopsgate
Elder St
Folgate St
Commercial St
Brick
OLD TRUMAN'S BREWERY
Earl St
Clifton St
Primrose St
Lamb St
Eagle St
Buxton St
Sun St
Appold St
DENNIS SEVERS HOUSE
Grey
Princelet St
Broadgate Circle
LIVERPOOL STREET
Brushfield St
Fournier St
Liverpool Street
Bishopsgate
Artillery La.
Fashion St
Liverpool St
New St
Middlesex
Bell La.
Wentworth St
Toynbee St
La.
Wormwood St
Heron Tower
Devonshire
Harrow Pl.
Goulston St
Gunthorpe St
WHITECHAPEL GALLERY
Old Broad St
Tower 42
St Helen's Bishopsgate
Bevis Marks
Houndsditch
Square
Aldgate East
Whitechapel High St
Leadenhall Building (Cheesegrater)
Mary Axe
The Gherkin
Botolph St
Aldgate
Leman St
Gracechurch St
Duke's Pl.
Aldgate High St
Leadenhall St
The Scalpel
Vine St
Jewry St
Alie St
Billiter St
Willis Building
Mansell St
Leadenhall Market
Lloyd's Building
FENCHURCH STREET
Minories
S Tenter St
Gracechurch
Portsoken St
Prescot St
The Walkie Talkie
Mincing Ln
ST OLAVE
Pepys St
Seething La.
TOWER GATEWAY
Chamber St
Fish St
St Mary-at-Hill
Pudding Ln
All Hallows-by-the-Tower
Tower Hill
Cartwright St
St Dunstan-in-the-East
Lower Thames St
TOWER OF LONDON
E Smithfield
Petty Wales
St Katharine's & Wapping
St Katharine's Way
THAMES
HMS BELFAST
English Grounds
Hay's La.
HAY'S GALLERIA
Tower Bridge
N

MUSEUM OF LONDON★★

G3 150 London Wall - ⊖ St Paul's or Barbican - ℰ020 7001 9844 - www. museumoflondon.org.uk - ♿ - 10h-18h (last admission 17h40) - closed 1st Jan and 24-26 Dec - free - guided tour £10 (45-60mn): at 11h, 12h, 15h and 16h.
An extraordinary museum in which the diversity of objects, reconstructions, films and models allow you to understand the history of London through technical progress, political changes or fashion. While the **London before London** section is dedicated to its first inhabitants, the five **Modern London** galleries retrace the evolution of the city, from the Great Fire of 1666 to the impact of the 2012 Olympics.

You can see the most beautiful **Roman frescoes** discovered in Britain, sculptures from the Mithra Temple, medieval pilgrimage medals, a model of the Rose Theatre and the **Cheapside Hoard** (Jacobean period jewellery),not to mention the diorama of the Great Fire, the doors from Newgate mansion, 19th century interiors and shops, the Lord Mayor's coach etc.

BARBICAN★

G3 ⊖ Barbican
Destroyed by bombs in the war, this area was completely reconstructed from 1958 as an austere architectural utopian complex, where pedestrians can walk on the upper level (car traffic at the lower level). A complex made of very particular concrete, where amateurs of brutalist architecture will roam between immense residential constructions, ornamental lakes, gardens and terraces before reaching **the Barbican Arts Centre**, a major location for London's cultural life (theatre, concert hall, art gallery, library, etc., www.barbican.org).

ST BARTHOLOMEW THE GREAT★★

G3 West Smithfield - ⊖ Barbican - ℰ020 7600 0440 - www. greatstbarts.com - ♿ - Mon-Fri 8h30-17h (16h from mid Nov to mid Feb), Sat 10h30-16h, Sun 8h30-20h - £5.
This church, is undoubtedly the most charming in London and is the only trace of an Augustinian priory for canons, dissolved in 1539. Built in 1123, it seduces by its eclecticism, a mix of Romanesque and Gothic architectures. The sobriety of the **choir** (12th century) is enhanced by a beautiful carved loggia. Note the **baptismal fonts** (15th), among the few surviving the Reformation in London, and over which the painter William Hogarth was blessed in 1697. The church appears in some scenes from the films Four Weddings and a Funeral and Shakespeare in Love and also houses contemporary works of art.

CHARTERHOUSE★

F/G3 Charterhouse Square - ⊖ Barbican - ℰ020 7253 9503 - www.thecharterhouse.org - Tues-Sun 11h-16h45 - free - guided tour £10 (1hr) on reservation Tues-Sun at 11h30, 13h45, 14h45.

Founded in 1371, this former Carthusian convent was turned into a Tudor mansion when Henry VIII dissolved the community and confiscated its buildings (1537). In 1611, the building was bought by **Thomas Sutton** (1532-1611), who established a boy's school and hospice for the poor. Charterhouse has undergone major architectural changes over the centuries, but you can still admire its splendid **Tudor Great Hall**, with frame diaphragms, woodwork and 16th century galleries. Its Elizabethan style **Great Chamber**, decorated with a monumental painted fireplace, gilded ceilings and leaded windows; or the **chapel** which has occupied the former capitulary room since 1614.
The museum offers a detailed retrospective view of history with period documents and even a skeleton of a victim from the Great Plague.

GUILDHALL★

G3 Gresham St. - ⊖ St Paul's - ☎020 7332 1313 - www.cityoflondon.gov.uk - 10h-16h30 - consult the website for closures.
Guildhall, a town hall in the City of London (not to be confused with that of the City of London) is the seat of the Corporation of London in charge of administering this area. It offers a majestic setting for lavish ceremonies. This building from the early 15th century miraculously survived the Great Fire of 1666, but underwent many more restorations following the 1940 Blitz. The impressive **Great Hall** with its vast proportions and superb oak ceiling, supported by stone

arches, was skillfully restored by Sir Giles Gilbert Scott. It is highlighted with a colourful frieze bearing the arms of England and the City, above which float the banners of the twelve major corporations (the Great Livery Companies) of the city. The hall retains some original features such as the exterior porch or stained glass of the south wall (first window to the right of the entrance). Among the monuments erected in honour of national figures, note on both sides of the gallery (called «Minstrels») to the west of the hall high wooden effigies of Gog (north) and **Magog** (south). These two legendary giants would have intervened in 1000 AD in the conflict between the Britons and the Trojan invaders. Erected in 1974 and Installed in the west wing, the library holds more than 14,000 works, documents and archives on London.

Guildhall Art Gallery and London's Roman Amphitheatre★
☎020 7332 3700 - www.cityoflondon. gov.uk (tab«Things to do/Guildhall Art Gallery») - 10h-17h, Sun 12h-16h (last admission 30 mins before closing) - closed 1st Jan and 25-26 Dec - free except exhibitions.
In the east wing of the courtyard, restored in the 1990s by Richard Gilbert Scott, this gallery holds some 250 pieces from the large art collection, exhibited in rotation, and acquired by the Corporation of London since the 17th century. It has nearly 4,000 works of art. In the basement, part of the remains of a **Roman amphitheatre** is visible.

ST MARY-LE-BOW ★★

G4 *Cheapside -* ⊖ *Mansion House -* ☎*020 7248 5139 - www.stmarylebow. co.uk - Mon-Wed 7h-18h, Thurs 7h-18h30, Fri 7h-16h.*

The protruding tower on Cheapside contains the famous **Bow bells** and supports the **majestic steeple★★** (1671-1680) where **Wren** used the five classical orders. A copper dragon installed by tightrope walkers serves as a weather vane. Completed in 1673, the Portland stone building built by Wren, which was inspired by the Basilica of Constantine in Rome, was bombed in 1941. The exterior was restored to the original while the interior was remodelled. The Romanesque **crypt**, built in 1087 on the ruins of a Saxon church, houses the original columns with cubic capitals. There is a restaurant on site (♨ *p. 118*).

ST MARGARET LOTHBURY ★

G3 ⊖ *Bank -* ☎*020 7726 4878 - www.stml.org.uk -* ♿ *- Mon-Fri 7h30-17h15.*

Part of the parish of the Bank of England, St. Margaret's church was built following **Wren**'s plans (1686-1690). The square tower is capped with an arrow that crowns a golden ball and **wind vane**.
Inside are beautiful **wood carved panels★**, benches, oak fences, a pulpit and altar. The elegant **rood screen★** comes from All Hallows Church (*Upper Thames St.*). The marble baptismal font is attributed to **Grinling Gibbons**.

BANK OF ENGLAND

G4 ⊖ *Bank (Lombard St. exit).*
Founded in 1694, the Bank of England marks the heart of the City. The actual building was built between 1924 and 1939 by Sir Herbert Baker to replace an older building by Sir John Soane.

Bank of England Museum★
Bartholomew Lane - ☎*020 7601 5545 - www.bankofengland.co.uk - Mon-Fri 10h-17h (last admission 16h30) - closed on p. holidays - free.*
It traces the history of the bank, from its foundation to the present day.

MANSION HOUSE ★

G4 ⊖ *Bank.*
Official residence of the first magistrate of the city, the Lord Mayor of London. Built between 1739 and 1752, it features a Palladian style facade punctuated by six Corinthian columns surmounted by a large triangular pediment.

ST STEPHEN WALBROOK ★

G4 *39 Walbrook -* ⊖ *Bank or Cannon St. -* ☎*020 7626 9000 - http:// ststephenwalbrook.net - Mon, Tues and Thurs 10h-16h, Wed 11h-15h, Fri 10h-15h30.*
This daring work by **Wren** (1672-1677) has a grey green **dome**. To the west, the rough stone square **tower** is surmounted by an elegant balustrade. The Portland stone **steeple** was added in 1717.
Inside, slightly off centre, the dome, rests on a ring of eight arches. The spans are marked by grouped

Sky Garden at the top of the Walkie Talkie designed by Rafael Viñoly

Corinthian columns to produce contrasts between the dark oak panelling and the light coloured wood carved furniture.

Note that the monumental travertine altar under the dome is the work of Henry Moore (1987).

ROYAL EXCHANGE★

G4 *Angle Threadneedle St. and Cornhill -* ⊖ *Bank.*
Neo-Classical in design, the former London Stock Exchange ceased operation in 1939. The building houses restaurants and luxury shops. On the esplanade in front of the monumental Corinthian portico facade, an equestrian statue of **Wellington** is erected.

LLOYD'S BUILDING★★ AND SURROUNDINGS

H4 *1 Lime St. -* ⊖ *Bank or Monument.*
Headquarters of the famous insurance group. It is similar to the Georges Pompidou Centre in Paris, which is hardly surprising since it is the work of **Richard Rogers**, one of the two Beaubourg architects. The avant-garde style of this stainless steel-clad concrete tower, which exposes its ducts and lifts in front to free up more of the interior space, was written about a lot on the occasion of its inauguration in 1986.

Just in front of the Lloyd's building, the **Willis Building** (*51 Lime St.*) stands out with its broad concave three tiered profile, reminiscent of

...ell. This 125m high
...r was designed by **Norman**
...

...ext door (*52-54 Lime St.*) is a new 190m high skyscraper called **The Scalpel**, due to its angular shape, designed by Kohn Pedersen Fox. On the other side of the junction stands the imposing **Leadenhall Building** (*122 Leadenhall St.*), named **The Cheesegrater** because of its slender prism shape. This achievement by **Richard Rogers**, Graham Stirk and Ivan Harbour, reaches 225m and was built in 2014.

WALKIE TALKIE★

H4 20 Fenchurch St. ⊖ Bank - skygarden.london - free, reserve online less than 3 days before - Mon-Fri 10h-18h, w/end 11h-21h.
At the southern end of Lime Street stands the massive and flared silhouette of this 160m building by Rafael Viñoly. A garden with panoramic terrace, **Sky Garden★★**, with bar and restaurant, is accessible on the 35th floor.

LEADENHALL MARKET★

H4 Access from Leadenhall St., Gracechurch St. and Lime St. - ⊖ Bank - ☏020 7487 1764 - www.cityoflondon.gov.uk (Tab «Things to do»/Leadenhall Market») - shops: Mon-Fri 9h-18h.
Formerly specializing in retail, this beautiful glass and wrought iron hall, with Victorian architecture, seems to resist change under neighbouring skyscrapers. Featured in the first **Harry Potter** movie, it is lined with shops, restaurants and pubs that fill up every Friday afternoon when the City's yuppies come to celebrate the end of the week.

THE GHERKIN★★ AND VICINITY

H4 30 St Mary Axe - ⊖ Bank or Aldgate.
«**The Gherkin**», as Londoners commonly call it, is the Swiss Re reinsurer's building and one of the great architectural successes of the London skyline. Designed by **Norman Foster** it was completed in May 2004. 100m north of the Gherkin, **The Heron Tower** (*110 Bishopsgate*) is 230m tall. Designed by Kohn Pedersen Fox and completed in 2011, is already generates electricity using solar panels. Two restaurants and a bar are located at the top (☾*Addresses / Nightlife p.141*). More classic, **Tower 42** (*25 Old Broad St.*), designed by Richard Seifert and erected in 1980, is already like a flower that's a little faded. Opposite, the construction work at **22 Bishopsgate** is suspended in time, but should start again soon to give rise to the tallest skyscraper in the city by 2019 (62 floors, 278m tall - more info. on at22.co.uk).

ST HELEN'S BISHOPSGATE★

H3 Great St Helen's - ⊖ Liverpool Street or Aldgate - ☏020 7283 2231 - www.st-helens.org.uk - ♿ - Mon-Fri 9h30-12h30.
The stone facade has a double pediment with crenelated gables; it is surmounted by a square turret

with lantern (17th century) crowned with a wind vane. Inside, the **funerary monuments**, opulent tombs of notables, earned it the nickname «Westminster Abbey of the City».

CANNON STREET

G4 ⊖ *Mansion House or Cannon St.* In the Middle Ages this street was called «Candelwriteystrete» (ie. Candlewright Street) because it was residence to manufacturers of candles and wicks. This explains the presence of the **candle manufacturers' premises** (*Tallow Chandler's Hall*) in Dowgate Hill and the former **skins and furs dealers** (*Skinner's Hall*), built at the end of the 18th century. In 1962 at No. 111, **London Stone**, a block of limestone was placed in the wall of the building (formerly home to the Bank of China), and came (according to legend) from the altar erected in 800 AD by Brutus of Troy, mythical founder of «insular Britain». In March 2016, planning permission was granted to demolish the building and replace it with a new one. The new premises will publicly display *London Stone* on a plinth, however until the work is completed the stone is on display at the Museum of London.

THE MONUMENT★

G4 *Fish St. Hill* - ⊖ *Monument -* ☎*020 7626 2717 - www. themonument.info - 9h30-18h (17h30 in winter), last admission 30 mins before closing - closed 24-26 Dec - £4.50, £11 ticket including admission to Tower Bridge.*

In 1667, the king entrusted **Wren** to design an impressive **Doric column** commemorating the Great Fire of London a year earlier. Its height (62m) represents the distance from the place where the fire first started, in Pudding Lane. Simply baptized «the Monument» by Londoners, provides a **panoramic view★** of the City from the viewing platform *(311 steps)*.

ST MARY-AT-HILL★★

H4 *The Rectory* - ⊖ *Monument -* ☎*020 7626 4184 - www.stmary-at-hill.org - Mon-Fri 10h-16h.*
The austere T shaped clocked facade and Venetian window of this church, built between 1670 and 1676 by **Wren**, hides an interesting interior architecture. His Greek cross **pattern★** is capped with a low dome supported by four Corinthian columns; the Adam style decoration is pastel blue and gold. Restored in 1843, but damaged by fire in 1988, the church was famous for its woodwork. Note, beneath a solid sounding board, the pulpit decorated with fruit and flowers is accessed by a curved 19th century staircase by **William Gibbs Rogers**.

57

Tower of London★★★

The romantic profile of the Tower of London, forever associated with the country's history, was as much the stage for horror scenes as it was for royal pomp. A visit to the Tower is imperative to admire the sparkling of the Crown Jewels and to take advantage of sombre narratives of «Yeomen Warders» in Tudor attire.

▶**Access:** 🚇 Tower Hill, Tower Gateway (DLR).
Map of area *p. 66-67.* **Detachable map** *H4-5.*
▶**Tip:** To visit the Tower of London, buy your ticket in advance to avoid long queues at the ticket office.

TOWER OF LONDON★★★

H4 *Access from West Gate -* 🚇 *Tower Hill - ticket office on the esplanade - 📞020 3166 6000 - www.hrp.org.uk - ♿ - Mar-Oct: 9h-17h30 Sun & Mon*

Guard and the cannons, Tower of London

© Pawel Libera/www.visitlondon.com

10h-17h30); Nov-Feb: 9h-16h30 (Sun & Mon 10h-16h30), last admission 30 mins before closing - guided tour accompanied by the London Yeomen Warders (1hr), departure every 30 mins from Middle Tower, last departure 15h30 (14h30 in winter) - closed 1st Jan and 24-26 Dec - £28 - audio guide (+£4).

It was to strengthen the defences of his new capital that **William the Conqueror** first built a wooden fortress here in 1067, which was replaced eleven years later by a stone building. Its advantageous position near the river provided a view of the enemies crossing the Thames. The successors of the Norman king knew how to appreciate this asset and enlarged the fortress, which soon filled 7 hectares.

Between 1300 and 1810, the Tower housed the Royal Mint, thanks to its fortifications, served as a prison and has become home to the **Crown Jewels★★★** since 1971; you will see a fabulous collection of jewels and royal insignia associated to the coronation, essentially after 1660, the largest part of the previous collection was sold or melted by Cromwell. Some of the Tower's torture victims are buried in the **Chapel Royal of St Peter ad Vincula** (*accessible during guided tours*), among which are Anne Boleyn and Catherine Howard. Notice the organ case sculpted by Grinling Gibbons.

Traitor's Gate was the Tower's main entrance when the Thames was still a major London traffic route. It took this name, later, when the river no longer served as a means of secret access. It is believed to be in the **Bloody Tower** that Edward IV's sons were murdered in 1483.

The keep, known as the **White Tower★★★**, is the most characteristic part of the Tower. It is one of the first fortresses of this size to be constructed in Western Europe. It was built by William I in 1078 and finished twenty years later. The 31 metre high stone walls form a quadrangle and, at the corners there is a circular tower and three square towers. The keep houses the **royal collection of armour**, one of the biggest in the world. **St John the Evangelist**'s two storey stone chapel★★ is located on the 2nd floor of the keep and is practically as it was in 1080. Robust columns with rough engraved capitals support the semi-circular arches which surround the choir, whose echo can be heard in the gallery above, under the dome.

Beauchamp Tower★, built in the 13th century, served as a prison for a long time. Note the graffiti engraved on the wall in the main room.

TOWER BRIDGE★★

H5 ⊖ *Tower Hill or London Bridge River Boat from Tower Pier - ☎020 7403 3761 - www.towerbridge.org.uk - ♿ - Apr-Sept: 10h-18h; Oct-Mar: 9h30-17h30, last admission 30 mins before closing - closed 24-26 Dec - £8.70; £12 ticket combined with Monument.*

The neo-Gothic silhouette and drawbridge of Tower Bridge are known around the world. Built between 1886 and 1894 by John Wolfe Barry and Horace Jones, its total length reaches 805m. Connected to the banks of the Thames by two suspension bridges, the massive Gothic towers that constitute the frame of the structure are joined together by a road bridge forming a drawbridge and, on the upper floor, by a pedestrian bridge, now equipped with a glass floor offering breathtaking **panoramic views★★★**. At 42m above the Thames, it forms a privileged observatory for the opening of the bridge.

The road bridge has two swinging decks to give passage to the ships. The manoeuvre lasts only a minute and a half and done several times a day. The hydraulic lifting mechanism has never failed however in 1977, it was replaced by a hydroelectric system.

Since 1992, the towers and engine room have housed an **educational centre**. From the north tower, the visitor is guided through an exhibition of the design and construction of the bridge.

Southwark★★

On the southern bank of the Thames, the large borough of Southwark is in full revival today. In the once notorious district of Bankside, the bustling Tate Modern, Norman Foster's Millennium Bridge and the Globe Theatre perfectly illustrates the successful marriage between history and modernity.

▶**Access:** London Bridge, Southwark.
Map of the area p. 66-67. Detachable map F/G/H4-5-6.
▶**Tip:** The entrance to the Tate Modern is free, so you should stagger your visit and not see everything the same day. Book online for The View from The Shard, tickets are cheaper than buying onsite. For lunch, enjoy stalls and restaurants at Borough Market or at the weekend, Maltby Street Market.

BUTLER'S WHARF

H5 London Bridge.
Luxury flats, cafes and restaurants on the riverbank have invaded this group of brick warehouses renovated in the 1980's.

CHINA WHARF

H5 London Bridge. Erected in 1988, over the waters of the Thames, this impressive building, festooned in orange-red hues, has earned its architects, **the CZWG group**, several awards. Other notable warehouse conversions include the **David Mellor Building** (*22-24 Shad Thames*), the modern **Saffron Wharf** (*18 Shad Thames*) and the untreated timber clad building, **the Camera Press**, (*21-23 Queen Elizabeth St.*).

MALTBY STREET MARKET

H6 41 Maltby Street, Ropewalk - Bermondsey - ✆079 7370 5674 - www.maltby.st - Sat 9h-16h, Sun 11h-16h.
Set up every weekend around the railway arches, the small gastronomic market of Maltby Street is proud of its

The Queen's Walk★★★

On the left bank of the Thames, The Queen's Walk is a long walk from Westminster Bridge to Southwark, Tower Bridge and beyond Bermondsey. South Bank (👣 p. 65) is the first part of this walk. On Bankside, Shakespeare's Globe Theatre (👣 p. 62) and the Tate Modern (👣 p. 64) are two iconic institutions that make the link between history and modernity. East of London Bridge Station, the bustling London Bridge City and beautiful Hay's Galleria Shopping Mall.

tempting selection of street food. If the offerings on the different stalls do not appeal to you, several restaurants can be found under the arches.

BERMONDSEY MARKET

H6 Angel Bermondsey St. and Long Lane - ⊖ *London Bridge - Fri 6h-14h.* Bermondsey's small **antique market** is a delight for strollers and early morning collectors. Amateur collectors of silverware will find a good choice of jewellery, cutlery, crockery, etc. The hallmark representing a lion indicates the object is of English origin.

CITY HALL

H5 The Queen's Walk - ⊖ *Tower Hill -* 𝄢*020 7983 4000 - www.london. gov.uk - Mon-Fri 8h30-18h.* The sparkling silhouette of this curved glass building (2002) was designed by **Norman Foster**. At its feet, an «arena» holds fine theatrical and choreographic performances.

HMS BELFAST

H5 The Queen's Walk - ⊖ *London Bridge -* 𝄢*020 7940 6300 - www.iwm.org.uk -* ♿ *- 10h-17h (last admission 1h before closing) - closed 24-26 Dec - £14.50 including audio guide.* Anchored upstream of Tower Bridge since 1971, this 11,500 tonne cruiser became noteworthy during the Second World War, in particular during the Normandy landing in 1944.

HAY'S GALLERIA

H5 Tooley St. - ⊖ *London Bridge.* Decorated with contemporary sculptures, this elegantly curved warehouse houses shops and cafés. Go from London Bridge station.

THE SHARD ★★

G5 Joiner St. - ⊖ *London Bridge -* 𝄢*084 4499 7111 - www.the-shard.com -* ♿ *- from start Apr to end Oct: 10h-22h (last admission 30 mins before closing); from end Oct to end Mar, Sun-Wed 10h-19h, Thurs-Sat 10h-22h (last admission 1hr before closing) - closed 25 Dec - £25.95 - reservation essential for the terrace: www.theviewfromtheshard.com.* Inaugurated in July 2012, the Shard is one of the last skyscrapers to rise up in the London skyline. Conceived by the architect Renzo Piano this glass building reaches 310 metres and is the tallest in London and Western Europe. Visitors can reach a **viewing platform★★★** 244 metres up, on the 72nd floor (*The View from the Shard*). The building also includes offices, a hotel, bars, restaurants and private flats.

BOROUGH MARKET

G5 8 Southwark St. - ⊖ *London Bridge - large market: Wed-Thurs 10h-17h, Fri 10h-18h, Sat 8h-17h - smaller market: Mon-Tues 10h-17h.* Nestled underneath the arches of a viaduct where three railway bridges form a triangle, this very lively major market is lined with pubs and small restaurants and consists of high end speciality products. ♿ *Addresses / Where to eat p. 114 /Shopping p. 132.*

SOUTHWARK CATHEDRAL★★

G5 London Bridge - ⊖ *London Bridge - ☏020 7367 6700 - cathedral. southwark.anglican.org - ♿ - Mon-Fri 8h-18h, w/end 8h30-18h - donation welcomed - guided tour (£3): Fri 11h & 13h, Sun 13h.*

The robust pillars support the central tower and Early English Gothic choir with harmonious proportions, dating back to the 13th century, making it the oldest Gothic sanctuary in England. It retains a sumptuous altar from 1520. The nave was rebuilt between 1890 and 1897 to harmonize with the **choir**. Note especially **Harvard Chapel** (*north aisle of the choir*), the funerary monument of Alderman Humble (1616), his wives (*north of the altar*) and twelve **keystones** from the 15th century timber structure which collapsed in 1830 (*west end of the north aisle*). The building also houses an archaeological room, an education centre, a cafeteria and shop.

GOLDEN HINDE

G5 Pickfords Wharf, Clink St. - ⊖ *London Bridge - ☏020 7403*

0123 - *www.goldenhinde.com - 9h30-18h - £7.*

Moored at St Mary Overie's Dock, the Golden Hinde is a life-size replica of Francis Drake's galleon. You can see the interior during a guided and costumed tour.

ROSE THEATRE

G4-5 21 New Globe Walk - ⊖ *Cannon Street or London Bridge - ☏020 7261 9565 - www.rosetheatre.org.uk - Sat 12h-16h.*

Part of the foundation from Bankside's first theatre (1587), were unearthed in 1989. The site can only be visited on Saturdays, but shows are regularly organized (*programme on website*).

SHAKESPEARE'S GLOBE★★

G4 21 New Globe Walk - ⊖ *London Bridge or Cannon Street - ☏020 7902 1500 - www.shakespearesglobe.com - ♿ - during theatre season (Apr.-Oct.): Mon-Sat 9h-12h30, Sun 9h-17h (dep. every 30 mins, except performances); out of season: everyday 9h-17h; exhibition: everyday 9h30-17h30; due to numerous events, check the calendar online - closed 24-25 Dec - £15 visit and exhibition of the*

Southwark's Yards and Inns

⊖ *London Bridge. A succession of alleys and yards sheltering inns, where travellers arriving in London lodged after the city doors were closed. By taking Borough High Street (back turned to Tower Bridge), you will discover **King's Head Yard**, **White Hart Yard**, **The George Inn**★; a picturesque inn portrayed by Dickens in «Little Dorrit», **Talbot Yard** or even **Queen's Head Yard**.*

Elizabethan theatre - restaurant, café.
In this place devoted to Shakespeare's
following, a replica of the Globe
Theatre, destroyed in 1644, was
built with materials and techniques
comparable to those of the time.
An ideal place for this circular
theatre, with the open air orchestra
surrounded by terraces, assisting
in the representation of one of
Shakespeare's plays, especially as,
for the sake of authenticity, the plays
are performed as in the days of their
author, in the afternoon and without
artificial lighting.

MILLENNIUM BRIDGE★

G4 ⊖ *Blackfriars.* Designed
by **Norman Foster**, the elegant
Millennium footbridge, suspended
and adorned with curved balustrades,
is a real feat of architecture and
technique. At night, it gives the
impression of a flow of light spanning
the Thames.

TATE MODERN★★★

F/G4 *Bankside -* ⊖ *Blackfriars -* ☏ *020
7887 8888 - www.tate.org.uk -* ♿ *-
10h-18h (Fri-Sat 22h), last admission
45 mins before closing - closed
24-26 Dec - free except temporary
exhibitions - free guided tours (45
mins): everyday at 11h, 12h, 14h, 15h,
see the programme on the website.*
The old «cathedral of the age of
electricity» built in 1960 on the
banks of the river, capped by a
glass superstructure and with large
projecting windows, has become
one of the world's temples of
contemporary art. The impressive
lobby is a former **turbine room**
(155m long and 35m high), where the
overhead travelling crane hints at the
industrial past of the building.
The substantial permanent
collections, are presented according
to a thematic approach, which owes
everything to the subjectivity of
the decision makers of the place.
Works of different eras are thus put
in parallel, historical and stylistic
associations are underlined so as to
question our accepted ideas about
contemporary art. The greatest
names in modern art, as well as all
the movements worth counting
are represented here; Picasso, Dalí,
Duchamp and his successors, Picabia
and Ernst, Twombly and Bacon,
Stella and Manzoni, Fontana, Klimt,
Cézanne, Rothko, Pollock and many
others interact freely in this immense
space.
In the basement, **The Tanks**, (former
oil tanks), have been converted into
a space dedicated to the living arts
(dance, performances, installations).
On the south side of the building, a
new 10-storey pyramidal extension,
designed by the architects Herzog
& de Meuron and named **The New
Tate Modern**, opened its doors in
June 2016. It thus increases the
exhibition area by 60% to welcome
the works of 250 artists from 50
different countries, including Mark
Rothko, Ai Weiwei, Louise Bourgeois
and Henri Matisse. You will also
find new educational and meeting
spaces, a shop, bar, restaurant and
terrace offering a superb **panoramic
view★★★** over London.

South Bank★★

*This area, which stretches between Waterloo and Blackfriars'
bridges, has forged a new identity with the development linked to festivities of
the third millennium. It is now a cultural and tourist centre.*

▶**Access:** ⊖ Southwark, Waterloo, Westminster, Lambeth North.
Map of the area p. 66-67. Detachable map E/F4-5-6.

OXO TOWER

F4 Barge House St. - ⊖ *Southwark or
Blackfriars - www.oxotower.co.uk.*
Dominated by a superb Art Deco
tower, this building was designed in
the 1900s as a power station before
being bought and remodelled by the
Liebig Company for the manufacture
of its famous Oxo stock cubes. Today,
the building houses art galleries,
artists' studios, fashion and design
boutiques, accommodation and a
panoramic restaurant.
♿ *Addresses /Where to eat p. 114/
Shopping p. 132.*

GABRIEL'S WHARF

F4 56 Upper Ground - ⊖ *Waterloo.*
Craft shops and cafes are brought
together around a pleasant square.

NATIONAL THEATRE★

F4-5 ⊖ *Waterloo - ☎020 7452 3000 -
www.nationaltheatre.org.uk -* ♿ *-
Backstage Tour, 1hr 15: see calendar
online - £10 .*
The National Theatre is part of
the third phase of the South Bank
development downstream of
Waterloo Bridge. Its architect, **Sir
Denys Lasdun**, has united three
theatres (the Olivier, the Lyttelton
and the Dorfman (formerly known as
the Cottesloe), with some 300 actors
and 500 costumes for about twenty
shows a year.

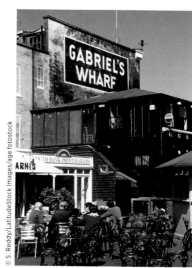

Gabriel's Wharf

© S. Reddy/LatitudeStock Images/age fotostock

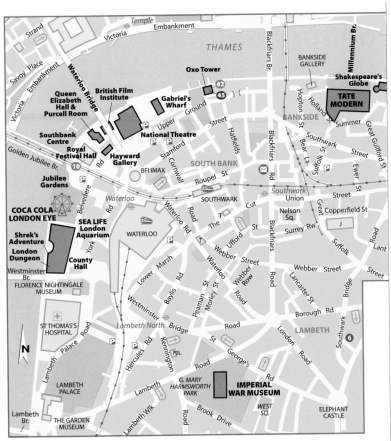

BRITISH FILM INSTITUTE

F5 ⊖ *Waterloo -* ℘*020 7928 3535/3232 - www.bfi.org.uk.*
Among the largest film libraries in the world, it has two theatres and organizes the London Film Festival.

WATERLOO BRIDGE

E4 ⊖ *Waterloo or Temple.*
The architect **Giles Gilbert Scott** designed this bridge in 1945 with five white Portland stone arches clad in reinforced concrete. It replaces

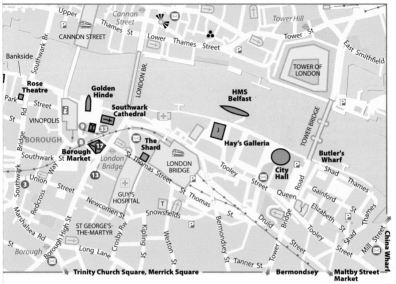

WHERE TO EAT		WHERE TO DRINK	
Arabica	9	George Inn (The)	13
Borough Market	8		
		SHOPPING	
Fish !	33	Borough Market	17
Oxo Tower		Oxo Tower Wharf	45
Restaurant & Brasserie	42		
		NIGHTLIFE	
Southbank Centre		Flat Iron Square	3
Food Market	10	Ministry of Sound	6

**SOUTHWARK
SOUTH BANK**

0	500 m
	500 yards

67

works inaugurated in 1817 for the 2nd anniversary of the Battle of Waterloo. On the banks sheltered by the bridge stands a **second-hand book market**. *(10h30-18h30)*.

SOUTHBANK CENTRE★

E5 *Belvedere Rd -* ⊖ *Waterloo -* ℘*020 3879 9555 - www.southbank centre.co.uk -* ♿.
For some, this group of buildings in stone and grey concrete, that

stands large and austere on the banks of the Thames, is a wart on the landscape. A symbol of brutalist architecture in the 1970s, London's most famous cultural complex has, in any case, quality programming and perfect acoustics. It includes three prestigious venues dedicated to classical or contemporary music and dance; **the Queen Elizabeth Hall** and **Purcell Room** (1967, *closed for restoration until 2018*), and especially the **Royal Festival Hall★** (1951, 10h-23h), a real architectural success in the industry. The latter brings together a 3,000 room concert hall with wonderful acoustics, a room devoted to chamber music, a ballroom and restaurant. The South Bank Centre also hosts contemporary art exhibitions at the **Hayward Gallery**.

JUBILEE GARDENS

E5 ⊖ *Waterloo or Westminster.*
Jubilee Gardens was created in 1977 to commemorate the Silver Jubilee of Queen Elizabeth II. This green space and the banks facing it are a very popular place.

COCA-COLA LONDON EYE★★★

E5 ⊖ *Waterloo - ✆0870 990 8883 - www.londoneye.com - ♿ - June - Aug: 10h-20h30; Sept-Dec: 11h-18h; Jan-Mar: 11h-18h; check opening times on the website - £22.45, cheaper tickets and fast track tickets can be bought online - possibility of ticket combined with SEA LIFE London Aquarium, London Dungeon, Shrek's*

Adventure and Madame Tussauds.
A true triumph of technology, this **big wheel**, 135m high and weighing 2,100 tonnes, has been a spectacular landmark on the banks of the Thames since 2000. For 30 minutes visitors in the 32 capsules discover an **exceptional view** 20km around.

COUNTY HALL

E5 Belvedere Rd - ⊖ *Waterloo or Westminster.*
This Classic style building (1912-1922) was the seat of the Greater London Council until it was abolished in 1986. It is home to various attractions (*combined ticket option, see Coca-Cola London Eye*).

London Dungeon

✆020 7654 0809 - www.the dungeons.com - ♿ - Mon-Fri 10h-17h (Thurs 11h), w/end 10h-18h, closes at 19h on public holidays (extended timetable Jul-Aug) closed 25 Dec - £30 - not advisable for sensitive people or young children. The visit (90 mins) of the London Dungeons is reserved for thrill seekers. A sinister review of the punishment inflicted on criminals, major epidemics, etc.

SEA LIFE London Aquarium★

*✆0871 663 1678 - www.visitsealife. com/london - ♿ - Mon -Fri 10h-18h, w/end and school holidays 9h30-19h (last admission 1hr before closing) - £26.*This submarine mecca goes down two storeys under the Thames. You will discover more than 500 different species distributed in 14 thematic zones.

County Hall and London Eye

Shrek's Adventure

✆0871 221 2837 - www.shreks adventure.com - ♿ - 10h-17h (Thurs 11h) - closed 25 Dec - £27.50.
Shrek and his companions are part of the latest Queen's Walk attractions. Spectators pass through several halls before meeting the green giant. Interest is limited for non-English speakers over 10 years old.

IMPERIAL WAR MUSEUM★★★

F6 Lambeth Rd - ⊖ Lambeth North - ✆020 7416 5000 - www.iwm.org.uk - ♿ - 10h-18h (last admission 17h30) - closed 24-26 Dec - free except certain exhibitions
This exceptional museum, with its collection and presentations, deals with the armed conflicts in which Great Britain and the Commonwealth have participated since 1914. The **First World War** is particularly well documented, with its models, dioramas and the reconstruction of a **trench** (*Level 0*). A section discusses daily life of a London family during the **Blitz** (*Level 1*). Further on, you will learn all about the different British intelligence services (*level 2*). Not recommended for children under 14. The exhibition on **the Holocaust** (*levels 3 and 4*) is one of the highlights of the visit because of its richness and the emotion it arouses. Finally, tribute is paid to 250 military and civilian heroes (*Level 5*).

Belgravia★★ and Knightsbridge★★

Luxury, peaceful and a sensual delight: Strolling around this most high end area of the capital is a feast for the eyes. If you are hooked on window shopping, it is a safe bet that your steps will lead you into department stores and chic and expensive boutiques - frequented by a wealthy and demanding public

▶**Access:** ⊖ Knightsbridge, Sloane Square.
Map of the area p. 72-73. Detachable map B/C5-6.

BELGRAVE SQUARE★★

C6 ⊖ *Knightsbridge.*
The square has preserved its original aspect with its central garden, lines

Sloane Street

© P. Robinson/age fotostock

of houses and detached mansions at the corners. Although it gives the appearance of great unity, colonnades and porticoes on each side present a different image, as well as the detached mansions.
From 1841-1870, the great statesman, Lord John Russell lived at No. 37 Seaford House in the East. The Queen's uncle, the Duke of Kent owned No. 3 (who died in 1942).

HARVEY NICHOLS

C5 *109-125 Knightsbridge -*
⊖ *Knightsbridge.*
Founded in 1813 and installed in 1880 at the current premises in Knightsbridge, this temple of luxury has, since then expanded worldwide.
♿ *Addresses /Shopping p. 132.*

HARRODS★★

B5 *87-135 Brompton Rd -*
⊖ *Knightsbridge.*
The most elegant department store in London, frequented by Oscar

Food halls, Harrods

Wilde, and rebuilt in 1849, but its current building dates only from the beginning of the 20th century. Inside the halls dedicated to food, glitter with mosaics and coloured stained-glass windows - a curious and rare example, as with Michelin House (♿ *p. 76*) of Art Nouveau in London. ♿ *Addresses / Shopping p. 132.*

BEAUCHAMP PLACE

B6 This street is home to elegant shops. At Nos. 56-57, a shop resembling the lounge of a mansion stands belonging to Caroline Charles, seamstress for the princesses.

SLOANE STREET

C5-6 The street, opened in 1773 to connect Knightsbridge to Chelsea and the Thames, was reconstructed gradually. **The Danish Embassy** (1976-1977) was designed by Arne Jacobsen. The western part of Sloane Street was known under the name of **Hans Town** (end of the 18th century).

CADOGAN SQUARE

B/C6 The shaded area of Cadogan Square and Cadogan Gardens, built at the end of the 19th century, owes its nickname «Dutch Street Bridge» to its tall red brick gabled houses, with white stone frames.

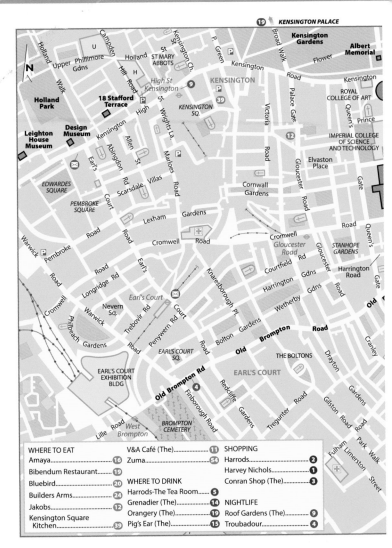

WHERE TO EAT		V&A Café (The) .... ⑪	SHOPPING	
Amaya .... ⑯		Zuma .... ㊿	Harrods .... ❷	
Bibendum Restaurant .... ⑲			Harvey Nichols .... ❶	
Bluebird .... ⑳		WHERE TO DRINK	Conran Shop (The) .... ❸	
Builders Arms .... ㉔		Harrods-The Tea Room .... ❺		
Jakobs .... ⑫		Grenadier (The) .... ⑭	NIGHTLIFE	
Kensington Square		Orangery (The) .... ⑲	Roof Gardens (The) .... ❾	
Kitchen .... ㊴		Pig's Ear (The) .... ⑮	Troubadour .... ❹	

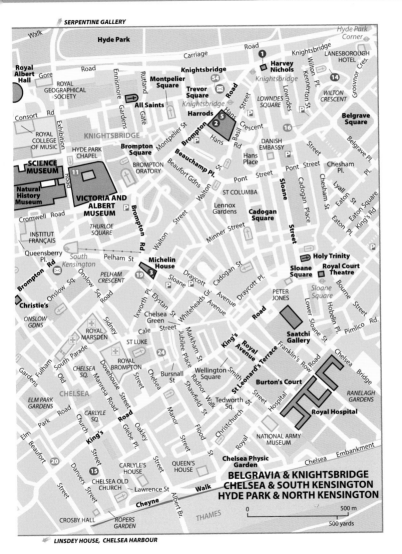

SERPENTINE GALLERY

Hyde Park

Hyde Park Corner

LANESBOROUGH HOTEL

Royal Albert Hall

ROYAL GEOGRAPHICAL SOCIETY

Knightsbridge

Harvey Nichols ❶

WILTON CRESCENT ⓮

Montpelier Square

Trevor Square 54

WILTON CRESCENT

Belgrave Square

All Saints

Harrods ❷ 5

DANISH EMBASSY

KNIGHTSBRIDGE

ROYAL COLLEGE OF MUSIC

HYDE PARK CHAPEL

Brompton Square

Beauchamp Pl.

Hans Place

Chesham Pl.

16

SCIENCE MUSEUM 11

BROMPTON ORATORY

ST COLUMBA

Natural History Museum

VICTORIA AND ALBERT MUSEUM

Lennox Gardens

Cadogan Square

INSTITUT FRANÇAIS

THURLOE SQUARE

Queensberry Pl.

South Kensington

Pelham St

Michelin House ❸ 19

Holy Trinity

Sloane Square

Royal Court Theatre

Christie's

ONSLOW GDNS

PELHAM CRESCENT

Sloane Square

PETER JONES

ROYAL MARSDEN

Chelsea Green

ST LUKE

Saatchi Gallery

ROYAL BROMPTON 24

Royal Avenue

Burnsall St

Wellington Square

St Leonard's Terrace

Burton's Court

RANELAGH GARDENS

CHELSEA

ELM PARK GARDENS

CHELSEA SQ.

Royal Hospital

CARLYLE SQ.

NATIONAL ARMY MUSEUM

20

CARLYLE'S HOUSE

QUEEN'S HOUSE

Chelsea Physic Garden

15

CHELSEA OLD CHURCH

Lawrence St

Cheyne Walk

**BELGRAVIA & KNIGHTSBRIDGE
CHELSEA & SOUTH KENSINGTON
HYDE PARK & NORTH KENSINGTON**

CROSBY HALL

ROPERS GARDEN

THAMES

0   500 m

500 yards

73

LINSDEY HOUSE, CHELSEA HARBOUR

Chelsea★★ and South Kensington★★

Along the beautiful streets of Chelsea, elegant and original shops, antique shops, stand alongside cafes and restaurants in a lively and «bobo» atmosphere. South Kensington, a leafy residential area lined with beautiful Victorian houses, is home to three of London's largest museums. Nicknamed «Froggy Valley» by Londoners, the area is home to a large French community built around the French Charles de Gaulle Lycée and French bookshops

▶**Access:** ⊖ Sloane Square, South Kensington and Gloucester Road.
Map of the area p. 72-73. **Detachable map** *A/B/C5-6-7-8.*

SLOANE SQUARE

C6 ⊖ *Sloane Square.* A square livened up, amongst others by **the Royal Court Theatre** (specializing in cutting edge avant-garde repertoire since 1870) and the Peter Jones store (1936). There is a commemorative plaque for William Willett, the inventor of summer (daylight saving) time.

HOLY TRINITY

C6 ⊖ *Sloane Square. Sloane St. - 𝄞020 7730 7270 - www.holytrinity sloanesquare.co.uk -* ♿ *- Mon - Fri 9h-18h, Sat 9h30-18h.*
Holy Trinity Church was rebuilt in 1888. It is **Burne-Jones**, stemming from the movement of the Pre-Raphaelites that designed 48 stained-glass windows for the choir. The decor and architecture accomplish a rare unity. Also notice the very delicate metalwork.

KING'S ROAD★

A8-B/C7 ⊖ *South Kensington.* This is a mecca for amateur shopping. Originally a simple path, King's Road owes its name to Charles II, who widened it to be able to get to Fulham quickly, where his lover Nell Gwynn lived. This big trading artery is known for its fashion shops, antique dealers, restaurants and pubs. Side streets situated in the north are lined with traditional houses built for craftsmen.

SAATCHI GALLERY

C7 Duke of York's HQ, King's Road - ⊖ *Sloane Square - 𝄞020 7811 3070 - www.saatchigallery.com - 10h-18h (last admission 17h30) - free - café, restaurant.*
Dedicated to contemporary art (painting, sculpture, video, installations) the 13 large rooms in this space are the setting for three to four exhibitions every year, most

frequently presenting unknown artists or those who have never exhibited in the United Kingdom.

ROYAL AVENUE

B/C7 ⊖ *Sloane Square.*
Planted with trees in the 17th century, this double avenue provides a view of the Royal Hospital's central pavilion creating a path cutting across **Burton Court**, limited to the north by St **Leonard's Terrace** (Georgian facades Nos. 14-31). James Bond fans probably know that the famous secret agent lives in Royal Avenue!

ROYAL HOSPITAL★★

C7 Royal Hospital Rd - ⊖ *Sloane Square* - ☎*020 7881 5200 - www. chelsea-pensioners.co.uk - Mon-Fri 10h-12h, 14h-16h.*
Founded in 1682 by Charles II in the style of Les Invalides that Louis XIV had built in Paris. It was then enlarged by James II, then by William and Mary, who entrusted the work to **Wren**. Note the main entrance, under its octagonal porch crowned with a lantern. War veterans (Chelsea Pensioners) are still here, as is the famous **RHS Chelsea Flower Show**. (♿ *p. 162*).

CHELSEA PHYSIC GARDEN★

B8 66 Royal Hospital Rd - ⊖ *Sloane Square* - ☎*020 7349 6458 - www. chelseaphysicgarden.co.uk -* ♿ *- Apr-Oct: Mon 11h-17h, Tues -Fri, Sun and public holidays: 11h-18h; Nov-Mar: Mon-Fri: 10h-16h (last admission 30 mins before closing) - £9.50 - café.*
Originally established by the Worshipful Society of Apothecaries, London's oldest botanical garden served as a testing ground for students. It follows a major research program.

CHEYNE WALK★

A/B8 ⊖ *Sloane Square.*
A pleasant walk along the Thames, when the traffic there is not too heavy. Lined with beautiful red brick houses where artists lived such as the writer **George Eliot** (No. 4), the poet and Pre-Raphaelite painter **D.G. Rossetti** (No. 16), the singer Mick Jagger (No. 48) or the painters Whistler (No. 96) and Turner (No. 119).

BROMPTON ROAD

B5-6 ⊖ *Knightsbridge or South Kensington.*
The triangle bounded by **Knightsbridge** and Brompton Road constitutes a typically Georgian residential area, organized around three squares; **Trevor Square** (1818), **Brompton Square** (1826) and **Montpelier Square★** (1837). The houses, with stucco ground floors and top floors in brick, are decorated with narrow windows and doors as well as magnificent balconies. Between these squares are an interlacing of alleyways, cottages in washed out colours (*Rutland Street*) and fences enclosing the small flower gardens. Although established shortly after the squares, **Ennismore Gardens** already has a Victorian style with

stucco mansions and rectangular pillar porches. The church of **All Saints**, built in Early English style, is now dedicated to Russian Orthodox worship.

MICHELIN HOUSE

B6 *81 Fulham Rd -* ⊖ *South Kensington.* Inaugurated in 1910, the first building in England to have a reinforced concrete structure, was occupied until 1985 by the tyre company Michelin. Its Art Nouveau decoration has been restored and the large tiled windows have been preserved, despite a considerable restructuring of the building. It now houses the **Conran Shop**. (⟁ *Addresses /Shopping p. 132*) and the **Bibendum Restaurant** (⟁ *Addresses /Where to eat p. 114*).

CHRISTIE'S

A6-7 *85 Old Brompton Rd -* ⊖ *South Kensington - www.christies.com.* Founded in 1766, this auction house enjoys international fame. It organizes sales in various fields (decorative arts, jewellery, photos, wines, etc.), amongst others, in New York, Paris, Geneva, Milan, Tel Aviv, Dubai or Hong Kong. The South Kensington Auction House is one of Christie's most active.

VICTORIA AND ALBERT MUSEUM★★★

B6 *Cromwell Rd -* ⊖ *South Kensington -* ☏*020 7942 2000 - www.vam.ac.uk -* ♿ *- 10h-17h45 (Fri 22h) - possibility of guided tours - closed 24-26 Dec - free except exhibitions - restaurant, cafés.*

The Victoria and Albert Museum, the national museum of decorative arts and design in Great Britain, was built to house the works that had been created for the 1851 World's Fair. In 1857, the collection was moved from Marlborough House to the South Kensington Museum. Later (1899), the museum was renamed in honour of the Queen, who laid the foundation stone of the current brick building. The early ill matched collection was then rapidly enriched with new acquisitions, today displaying fine and applied arts from all countries, styles and periods (2 million objects, 10km of galleries).

Even those who are allergic to museums will find their happiness in the 'V & A', as Londoners call it. You can admire the national collection of furniture, British sculptures, textiles, ceramics, silverware and watercolours, from 1500 to 1900; but also sculptures from the Italian Renaissance, Islamic art rugs, Japanese lacquers or contemporary glass art work, among countless works from all civilizations and eras.

It will not be possible to discover everything in one visit. Therefore finding yourself in this proliferation of objects, arm yourself with a map and head to the rooms that naturally attract you to the geographical area or era they cover.

The museum's new entrance is on Exhibition Road, facing the Science and Natural History museums. It opens on to Sackler Courtyard, a vast patio lined with a café and shop,

Hintze Hall, Natural History Museum

and leads underground, to the huge Sainsbury Gallery and conservation workshops

NATURAL HISTORY MUSEUM★★

A/B6 Cromwell Rd - ⊖ South Kensington - ℰ020 79 42 50 00/11 - www.nhm.ac.uk - &. - 10h-17h50 (last admission 17h30) - closed 24-26 Dec - free except exhibitions - themed evenings and «dinosaur» nights for adults or children (calendar and reservations on website) - restaurant, cafés.

Alfred Waterhouse's grand palace, inspired by the medieval architecture of Rhineland, has housed the national Natural History museum since 1881, which came into existence through donations from private collections. The Irish naturalist and collector **Sir Hans Sloane** (1660-1753) bequeathed more than 80,000 specimens of animals, plants, stones and minerals amassed during his lifetime. Botanist **Joseph Banks** (1740-1820) on the other hand gave up the herbarium built in 1768-1771 on his voyage around the world alongside Captain James Cook. The museum was later enriched with collections from the East India Company (1858), the Zoological Society of London (1938) and, more recently, the Geological Museum (1985). Today, the collection illustrates all forms of life, from the smallest bacteria to the largest creature, including fossils and dinosaurs, minerals and rocks. The main building on Cromwell Road is home to the Life Galleries and the Darwin Centre, a high-tech, evolutionary design. The Exhibition Road building houses the Earth Galleries.

Worth knowing: the replica of diplodocus' impressive skeleton, usually displayed in Hintze Hall and known as 'Dippy', is on tour until 2020. A whale replaces it.

SCIENCE MUSEUM★★★

A/B6 Exhibition Rd - ⊖ *South Kensington -* 𝒫*0870 870 48 68 - www.sciencemuseum.org.uk -* ⚒ *- 10h-18h; school hols: 10h-19h (except last Wed of the month 18h), last admission 45 mins before closing; themed evenings for adults every last Wed of the month (except Dec) - closed 24-26 Dec - free except flight simulators, IMAX cinema, Discovery Motion Theatre, Wonderlab and certain exhibitions - restaurant, cafés.*

This laboratory/factory of human inventions spans nearly 3 hectares. A temple of sciences, this museum is remarkable in many ways; for the diversity of its collections - more than 10,000 exhibits, some priceless, covering the entire western history of science, technology and medicine - and for the quality of its educational exhibitions which favours interactivity. It is obvious that you cannot visit six floors of the museum in one day. So it is preferable to select the themes which interest you in the welcome guide (at reception) before you go to discover countless scale models, to pull levers, push buttons or conduct experiments yourself.

Among the most popular areas;

the **Flight Gallery**, dedicated to the progress of air transport; the **Fly Zone**, where the young and old can experiment with different **flight simulators** (*for a fee*), and the brand new interactive gallery **Wonderlab** (*paying*), where youngsters can try out the job of a scientist. The Wellcome Wing is home to the **IMAX Theatre** and the **3D Theatre Discovery Motion** (*paying*), as well as the **Antenna Gallery** and its temporary exhibition dedicated to science, medicine and technology news, which distracts visitors by stimulating their imagination. If you are in a hurry, visit the following galleries: Build the Modern World (*Ground Floor*), Antenna (*Wellcome Wing, Ground Floor*), Unexpected Materials (*1st Floor*), Flight (*3rd Floor*) and Scenes from Medical History (4th Floor).

ROYAL ALBERT HALL★

A5 ⊖ *South Kensington, Knightsbridge -* 𝒫*020 7589 8212 - www.royalalberthall.com - Possibility of guided tour.*

The Albert Hall was designed by Captain Fowke, a royal engineer. Circular in shape, built in red brick, with a metal dome, it represents the exact opposite of the **Albert Memorial** (♿*p.80*), both in form and ornamentation. Its unique decoration consists of a terracotta frieze evoking the Triumph of Arts and Sciences. Dedicated to extremely diverse activities, for eight successive weeks in the summer, it is the setting of the famous Proms or concert-walks, which attract up to 7,000 spectators at a time (♿*p.162*).

Hyde Park★★ and North Kensington★★

True green lungs of the capital, Hyde Park and Kensington Gardens together form the biggest public garden of the city. All year round, Londoners go to cycle or rollerblade there, to run, row or listen to a concert. With its beautiful houses decorated with white stucco, and commercial streets lined with elegant shops, North Kensington is proud of its aristocratic connections. It provides a happy alternative to Knightsbridge and Oxford Street for amateur shoppers.

▶**Access:** ⊖ Marble Arch, Hyde Park Corner, Lancaster Gate, Queensway, Bayswater, High Street Kensington, Notting Hill Gate, Holland Park.
Map of area p. 72-73. **Detachable map** *ABC4-5.*

HYDE PARK★★

BC4-5 ⊖ *Marble Arch or Queensway. From 5h to 0h - www.royalparks.org.uk.*
To the east of Serpentine Bridge and West Carriage Drive, this large park attracts Londoners with the slightest ray of sun. In the summer, you can listen to orchestras there, canoe on the Serpentine, ride horses and practice your golfing skills.
At the northeast corner of Hyde Park rises **Marble Arch**, a white marble triumphal arch designed in 1827 by **John Nash** to mark the main entrance to Buckingham Palace. Finding it too narrow to let the coaches pass, it was dismantled and rebuilt here, on the spot where the Tyburn gibbet once stood.

© Stéphane Frances/hemis.fr

Hyde Park

Not far away, **Speakers' Corner** is a place of public debate instituted in 1872, testifying to the freedom of expression of the British. Southwest of the park, **the Princess Diana Memorial** Fountain was re-opened in 2004.

KENSINGTON GARDENS★★

A4-5 ⊖ *Queensway or Lancaster Gate.* Kensington Gardens were most beautiful under Queens' Mary, Anne and Caroline (George II's wife) with Royal Gardeners Henry Wise and his successor, Charles Bridgeman in 1728. It was in the 18th century when the Round Pond was created, from where avenues radiate towards the Serpentine and the Long Water. Another achievement of this period, the **Orangery★**, which houses a restaurant and tea room. Note: The Orangery is now closed but the palace cafe is open for refreshments. (🍴 *Addresses / Where to drink p. 126).*

Serpentine Gallery

To the southeast of Kensington Gardens - ☎*020 7402 6075 - www. serpentinegallery.org - &. - Tues- Sun and public holidays 10h-18h - restaurant, tea room.* This attractive pavilion holds quality contemporary art exhibitions. **The Serpentine Sackler Gallery**, an annexe fitted out by Zaha Hadid, opened in 2013 on the other side of the Serpentine and includes a restaurant. (🍴 *Addresses / Where to eat p. 114).*

Albert Memorial★

Inaugurated in 1876, it rises at the top of four flights of stairs, its neo-Gothic arrow designed by George Gilbert Scott. In the centre, surrounded by allegorical statues and a frieze of 169 effigies of artists (composers, architects, poets, painters, and sculptors) and enthroned, a golden bronze statue of the husband of Queen Victoria, promoter of the Arts and Education. Prince Albert (1819-1861) in particular is at the origin of the great museums in Kensington, an area, at one time nicknamed «Albertopolis».

KENSINGTON PALACE★

A5 Kensington Gardens - ⊖ *Queensway or High Street Kensington -* ☎*0844 482 7799 - www.hrp.org.uk - &. - 10h-18h (Nov-Feb: 16h), last admission 1hr before closing - closed 24-26 Dec - £19.* Since its acquisition in 1689 by William III, this house from the beginning of the 17th century has known three periods; under the house of Orange, it was the private residence of the monarch and **Wren** was the main architect; under the first Hanovers, it became Palace Royal, decorated by Campbell and Kent; since 1760, it has been a residence reserved for members of the Royal Family. Queen Victoria, to whom a room is completely dedicated, lived there, as well as the Prince of Wales and Princess Diana. It's obvious that the Royal Family uses the crown as the main subject for the exhibition. Clothes of ceremony, objects and paintings form the main part of the Collections.

18 STAFFORD TERRACE★

A5 18 Stafford Terrace - ⊖ High Street Kensington - ✆020 7602 3316 - www.rbkc.gov.uk (tab« Leisure and Culture/Our museums ») - free visit: Wed, w/end 14h-17h30 - £7; guided tour: Wed & Sun (traditional), Sat (costumes), 11h-12h15; 3ʳᵈ Thurs of the month (Twilight Evenings), 19h - £10-12.

The famous illustrator **Linley Sambourne** (1844-1910) moved into this house in 1875 and began to redecorate it in Aesthetic style, popular at the time. The rooms have retained their original decoration and furniture.

HOLLAND PARK★

A6 Access from Kensington High St., Abbotsbury Rd & Holland Park Ave. - ⊖ Holland Park or High Street Kensington - from 7h30 to 30 mins before sunset.

This beautiful 22 hectare park is very popular with London families, who appreciate the tranquillity of its shaded paths, Japanese garden, children's games and many sports facilities.

DESIGN MUSEUM★★

A6 224-238 Kensington High St. - ⊖ High Street Kensington - ✆020 7940 8790 - www.designmuseum.org - ♿ - 10h-18h (last admission 17h), evenings 1ˢᵗ Fri of the month 20h - closed 25-26 Dec - free except temp. exhibitions - café, restaurant.

Opened in November 2016, this impressive 10,000m² space deserves a visit especially for its top floor, where you will discover the evolution of contemporary design with the permanent «Designer Maker User» collection, which exhibits key objects from each of the main areas of design (housing, transport, IT, automotive, textile, etc.). The temporary exhibitions are on the ground floor, next to the café and the shop. Feel free to sit on the steps, or in the lobby, to admire the parabola-shaped ceiling.

81

LEIGHTON HOUSE MUSEUM★

A6 12 Holland Park Rd - ⊖ High Street Kensington - ✆020 7602 3316 - www.rbkc.gov.uk (tab «Leisure and Culture») - every day except Tues 10h-17h30 (last admission 17h) - closed 1st Jan and 25-26 Dec - guided tour Wed & Sun 15h - themed evening one Fri a month - £9.

This house, built in 1866 by Lord Leighton (1830-1896), a Victorian painter and president of the Royal Academy, is a perfect reflection of the Victorian style of his installations.

Notting Hill★★ *and Little Venice*

The raspberry pink, canary yellow, water green, royal blue facades and peaceful Notting Hill mews' make up one of London's most beautiful postcards. Around Portobello Road, the main street, there is a succession of restaurants, bobo cafés, elegant designer boutiques and artists' galleries, not to mention the famous flea market which, at the end of the week, attracts hordes of bargain hunters in search of old records, a trinket or antique furniture. There are many people due to its success, but just take the side roads to savour the chic village atmosphere of Notting Hill. Enthusiasts looking for second hand or vintage objects will find them to the north of the area which is more real and less touristy.

▶**Access:** ⊖ Notting Hill Gate, Ladbroke Grove, Paddington.
Map of Notting Hill see opposite. Little Venice on the Detachable map at A2-3.
▶**Tip:** Fri-Sat are the best days to visit Portobello market.

PORTOBELLO ROAD★

A3 ⊖ *Notting Hill Gate, Ladbroke Grove.*
This winding street, formerly a cross-country road from the Notting Hill toll Gate, comes alive on Friday and Saturday when the **flea market** is on (*9h-17h*). At the end of August, Portobello Road is **Notting Hill Carnival's** (⏺ *p. 162*) assembly point. From Chepstow Villas to the intersection with Lonsdale Road, there is a succession of antique shops interspersed with sophisticated restaurants. The atmosphere becomes more real as you head north, especially near **Golborne Road**, where antique shops sit side by side with pleasant cafés, grocery stores, Moroccan and Portuguese bakeries in an almost Mediterranean atmosphere.

KENSINGTON PARK ROAD

A3 ⊖ *Ladbroke Grove.*
Kensington Park Road rivals Portobello Road in terms of liveliness. Bars and restaurants are open late at night there.

LITTLE VENICE

A2-3 ⊖ *Warwick Avenue - on Bloomfield Rd, to the west of Edgware Rd.*
Little Venice is an attractive triangular basin bordered by weeping willows, at the junction of Regent's Canal and Paddington Basin. Its waters reflect Georgian mansions interspersed with modern buildings and a former toll house (now a pub). This is the starting point for canal walks to Camden via Regent's Park Zoo. (⏺ *p. 89, p. 94 & p. 158*).

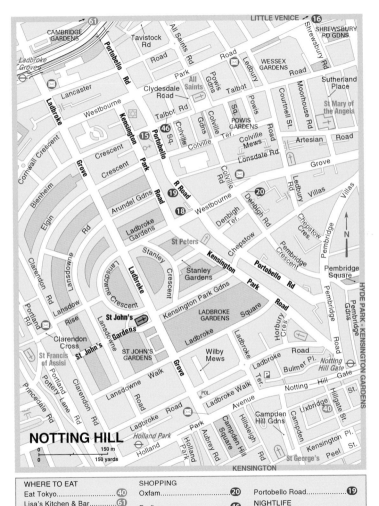

83

Marylebone★ and Regent's Park★★★

No need to be called Sherlock Holmes to guess that Oxford Street, the longest trading artery in the world, and nearby streets lined with elegant shops, is a real paradise for window shoppers. But Marylebone's very rich area provides pleasant surprises for the walker who wanders off to explore its alleys and quiet public gardens, where magnificent 18th century houses are nestled, one of them housing the treasures of the Wallace Collection. To escape the urban jungle drastically you need to head further north towards the very beautiful greenery of Regent's Park.

▶**Access:** ⊖ Regent's Park, Great Portland Square, Baker Street, Marble Arch, Bond Street.
Map of the area p. 87. Detachable map B/C/D1-2-3-4.
▶**Tip:** If you plan on visiting Madame Tussauds, buy your ticket in advance to avoid the long queues.

84

OXFORD STREET★

C/D3-4 ⊖ *Bond Street.* Oxford Street.
It extends eastward as far as Marble Arch and the outskirts of Hyde Park. A shopping street «par excellence», it is home to the famous and impressive **Selfridges** store at No. 400, built in 1908 by Gordon Selfridge; with immense Ionic columns on three levels joined to a roof terrace with a balustrade, and an entrance protected by a canopy. Other department stores along the street: John Lewis, D.H. Evans, Debenhams, Marks and Spencer, etc. To the east the artery reconnects with Bloomsbury (🕭 *p. 90*).

THE SQUARES★

B/C3 ⊖ *Baker Street.*
Gloucester Place lures you with its small alleys and wrought iron balconies. **Montagu Square**, which dates from the early 19th century, is lined with residences whose ground floors are lit by small bow windows. Anthony Trollope lived here at No. 39 (1873-1880). **Bryanston Square**, which dates from the same period, is adorned with stucco terraces.
At the northeast corner of **Portman Square** remain two of the most beautiful houses that have ever occupied the square (Nos. 20 & 21). The first, built by **Robert Adam** between 1772 and 1777, was intended for Elizabeth, Countess of Hume.

Oxford Circus

St Christopher's Place is a charming pedestrian area well known for its outdoor cafés and small shops.

WALLACE COLLECTION★★★

C3 *Hertford House, Manchester Square -* ⊖ *Bond Street -* ☏ *020 7563 9500 - www.wallacecollection.org -* ♿ *- 10h-17h - closed 24-26 Dec - free - audio guide £4 - guided tours: 11h30, 13h and 14h30 according to the day - restaurant, café.*

In the heart of Marylebone, on a Georgian square, **Hertford House** is home to the superb collection of French art accumulated by the 4th Marquis of Hertford (1800-1870), who lived most of the time at Bagatelle Castle in the Bois de Boulogne, Paris. In the family collection of Italian masters and 17th century Dutch paintings, he added 18th century French furniture, Sèvres porcelain, as well as paintings by **Watteau**, **Boucher** and **Fragonard**. His natural son, **Richard Wallace** (1818-1890), who endowed Paris with fountains bearing his name, increased the collection further, which he transferred to England and in 1900 it was donated to the British nation by his widow.

On the ground floor is the gallery dedicated to the Renaissance with works combining sculptures and paintings from Italy, France and

Flanders. Then come vast rooms displaying ancient European and Oriental weapons. On the first floor, **the Great Gallery★★**, which has regained all its splendour, brings together the biggest 17th and 18th century paintings, among others **Titian**'s *Perseus and Andromeda*, The Lady with a fan by **Velázquez**, two impressive full length portraits; *Philippe Le Roy* by **Van Dyck**, **Frans Hals**' superb *laughing Cavalier* (he is not a rider and he only sketches a vague enigmatic smile), **Rubens**' *The Rainbow Landscape*, whose counterpart is at the National Gallery; several religious paintings including **Murillo**'s *Adoration of the Shepherds*, and a moving portrait of his son *Titus* by **Rembrandt**, but also works by Nicolas Poussin, Philippe de Champaigne and English portrait painters Thomas Gainsborough and Thomas Lawrence. Beautiful sumptuously adorned rooms also give pride of place to the rich and colourful 18th century French paintings (Greuze, Boucher, Fragonard).

MADAME TUSSAUDS★

C2 Marylebone Rd - ⊖ Baker Street - ☏0 870 400 3000 - www.madame-tussauds.com - variable timetable according to the days and months (last admission 1hr 30 before closing) - £29 (reduced rate and fast track ticket on the website) - possibility of ticket combined with the Coca-Cola London Eye and South Bank attractions (♿ p. 65).

The famous waxworks museum includes the French royal family (Louis XVI and Marie-Antoinette) made by Mrs. Tussaud herself, the effigies of illustrious figures from all countries and eras, as well as statesmen, sportsmen and artists or English murderers, sometimes staged in very realistic surroundings.

SHERLOCK HOLMES MUSEUM

C2 221B Baker St. - ⊖ Baker Street - ☏020 7224 3688 - www.sherlock-holmes.co.uk - 9h30-18h - closed 25 Dec - £15.

Recognize that it is amazing to dedicate a museum to someone who has never existed. We enter the Victorian flat where Sherlock Holmes and Dr. Watson «lived» between 1881 and 1904, put together according to the descriptions gleaned from the pages of Sir Arthur Conan Doyle's novels. A visit recommended for enthusiasts, who will recognize the predictable outfit: cap, pipe, magnifying glass, but also clues, exhibits and murder weapons from the adventures of the famous stooge.

REGENT'S PARK★★★

C1-2 ⊖ Regent's Park - www.royalparks.org.uk - variable timetable according to the season.

At the beginning of the 19th century, vast lands which had been allotted by Cromwell to various farmers were surrendered to the Crown, who decided to have them developed. At that time major large scale property deals were common and it was **Nash** who developed the plan for the new neighbourhood, which was only partly

MARYLEBONE AND REGENT'S PARK

0   500 m
0   500 yards

London Zoo

REGENT'S PARK

Albert Road

Circle

Outer

Circle

Delancey St

Camden High

Crowndale St

Parkway

Mornington
Crescent

Eversholt St

Village East

Hampstead Road

Euston

REGENT'S
PARK

Robert St

Terraces

Terraces

Albany Street

ST JOHN'S
WOOD

Prince Albert Road

Outer

Canal

OPEN AIR
THEATRE

Inner

Chester Rd

Euston Square

P

Regent's
Boating
Lake

Queen Mary's
Gardens

Regent's
College

Circle

POL.

Euston Road

Terraces

MARYLEBONE

Park Road

Terraces

Sherlock Holmes
Museum

Ulster

Terrace

Regent's
Park

Great
Portland
Street

Euston

Warren
Street

Lisson

Rossmore Rd

Clenworth

Ulster

Road

FITZROY
SQ.

Cleveland Street

Broadley St

Grove

Marylebone

Baker
Street

Madame
Tussauds

Devonshire Street

Wimpole
St

Harley

Portland
Place

Great Portland Street

BRITISH
TELECOM
TOWER

87

Edgware
Road

Marylebone

Paddington St

Newman St

Crawford St

Gloucester
Place

Baker
St

New

Cavendish
St

ALL SOULS
CHURCH

12

Mortimer
Street

Wells
St

Great Castle
St.

Bryanston
Sq.

60

21

WALLACE
COLLECTION

55

St

Marylebone
La.

CAVENDISH
SQ.

Regent St

Sussex Gdns

Edgware

Montagu
Sq.

66

Thayer St

22

Wigmore

P

George

MANCHESTER
SQ.

James St

St Christopher's
Place

Oxford Circus

Street

Kendal St

Portman
Sq.

Duke

Oxford

Bond
Street

HANOVER
SQ.

LIBERTY

Great Marlborough St

N

Connaught St

Seymour

Road

St

Orchard
St

Selfridges

Street

Conduit St

Regent

Beak. St

Marble
Arch

Bayswater Road

Upper Brook Street

GROSVENOR
SQ.

Brook Street

New Bond St

Savile
Row

Old Bond St

Heddon St

Vigo St

The Ring

Hyde

Mount Street

South Audley Street

BERKELEY
SQ.

MAYFAIR

Curzon Street

Albemarle St

Dover St

ROYAL
ACADEMY
OF ART

Park

Park
Lane

Piccadilly

Jermyn St

Green Park

LORD'S CRICKET GROUND CLUB

built between 1817 and 1825. Neither the villas, nor the pantheon, nor its halo of buildings came into being. The inner ring road, **Inner Circle**, surrounds an old botanical garden, now transformed into a flower garden, **Queen Mary's Gardens**, which includes an open-air theatre. Outside The Inner Circle, The Holme is one of Nash's rare villas, while **Regent's College** occupies another one, rebuilt and enlarged in the 20th century.

Outer Circle, however, a ring road on the periphery of the park is in line with the project. Three of its external edges are lined with splendid **palaces★★** constituting terraces.

Park Crescent near Regent's Park created by John Nash

© J. Castle/Loop Images/age fotostock

THE «TERRACES» TO THE WEST OF OUTER CIRCLE★★

B/C2 ⊖ *Regent's Park. Walk in a clockwise direction.*

Park Crescent (1821) is a graceful Classic-style hemicycle designed by **Nash** to connect Portland Place to Regent's Park. The buildings (1823-1824) forming the east and west wings of **Park Square** are adorned with a simple Ion-style colonnade.

Ulster Terrace (1824) can be recognized by its two pairs of adjoining bay windows at each end of the building.

Spreading out almost 330m (half the width of the park), **York Terrace** (1821) consists of two symmetrical blocks arranged around York Gate and some annexed houses. Villas, adorned with imposing Corinthian columns frame the central body, while the York Gate houses are Ionic style.

Cornwall Terrace (1822) is a long building (170m) with Corinthian colonnades designed to create an elusive perspective.

The central part and angles of **Clarence Terrace** (1823) have heavy Corinthian pediments on an Ion arcade.

Sussex Place (1822) is a curved building, home to the London Graduate School of Business Studies, which is surprisingly towered by peak-shaped domes, connected by an array of Corinthian columns. The Royal College of Obstetrics and Gynaecology is housed in a brick building built in 1960.

The pale blue pediments of **Hanover Terrace** (1823) serve as a background to a plaster frieze and pedestal for statues standing out against the sky. Behind a small octagonal pavilion, at Hanover Gate stands the **mosque** (1977), with its white minaret surmounted by a golden dome and thin crescent. Designed by **Sir Frederick Gibberd**, its light grey facade is opened by tall, five-mullioned windows. Other modern buildings house the Islamic Cultural Centre.

Hanover Lodge consists of a row of modern villas (1989) harmonizing with an 18th century villa.

THE «TERRACES» TO THE EAST OF THE OUTER CIRCLE ★★

C1-2 ⊖ *Regent's Park.*
Cambridge Terrace (1825) was restored at the same time as the nearby buildings, while **Cambridge Gate** (1875) remains a fully Victorian building with pavilion roofs. The latter stands on the site of the former Colosseum, a large rotunda where exhibitions and slideshows took place. **Chester Terrace** (1825) has the longest uninterrupted facade (286m) with imposing Corinthian columns. At each end, triumphal arches open onto the interior access road.
Cumberland Terrace (1826) has a monumental facade, with Ionic columns that almost rival the previous one (242m long). The carved central pediment, which parallels that of Hanover Terrace, is topped with allegorical statues from the Arts and Science of England.

The main part of Gloucester Gate (1827) is flanked by stucco porticoes, contrasting with the red of the tympana and statues lost in the sky. Cross the gate and make a detour to Albany Street to see **Park Village West**. Smaller terraces, smaller houses, and Nash-style cottages give a provincial look to a lovely horseshoe-shaped street.

LONDON ZOO ★★

C1 Regent's Park, Outer Circle - ⊖ *Camden Town - possibility of accessing by boat via Regent's Canal - ☎0344 225 1826 - www.zsl.org - ♿ - Open at 10h, closes according to the season (last admission 1 hr before closing) - closed 25 Dec - variable tariff according to season, from £24.30 (reduced tariff and fast track tickets available on the website) - restaurant, cafeteria.*
In 1828, the Zoological Society of London opened the zoo on a 2 hectare plot. It currently covers 14. Eight thousand animals of 900 species are exhibited. The Zoological Society continues to play a leading role in the protection of endangered species by studying their breeding conditions in particular, while improving the living conditions of animals in zoos.

Bloomsbury★

Bloomsbury is home to beautiful 18th and 19th century squares, lined with Georgian and Victorian houses. Formerly greatly prized by artists and writers, this residential area was, at the beginning of the 20th century, the cradle of the Bloomsbury Group, to which Virginia Woolf belonged. Big institutions, such as the British Museum and University of London immortalize this artistic and intellectual tradition.

▶**Access:** ⊖ Tottenham Court Road, Goodge Street, Russell Square.
Detachable map D/E2-3.
▶**Tip:** The British Museum is huge, do not plan a programme that's too ambitious. Why not take one of the many free thematic guided tours available every day?

BEDFORD SQUARE★★

D/E3 ⊖ *Tottenham Court Road.*
The most beautiful and best kept squares in Bloomsbury was converted from 1775 by the architect Thomas Leverton. The three storey brick houses have doors, topped with elegant half-moon windows, and balconies raised by a central stucco pediment on the first floor.

BRITISH MUSEUM★★★

E3 *Great Russell St. -* ⊖ *Tottenham Court Road or Holborn -* ✆*020 7323 8299 - www.britishmuseum.org -* ♿ *- 10h-17h30 (Fri 20h30) - guided tour: programme at entrance and on website - closed 1st Jan and 24-26 Dec - free except some exhibitions - multimedia guide £6 - restaurant, cafés.*
If the oldest of the world's national museums (1759) presents jewels

of Western art, it deserves a visit especially for its antique and ethnographic collections. Don't miss the Egyptian antiquities, with the famous **Rosetta stone** that allowed Champollion to decipher hieroglyphs. Large rooms are reserved for the **Parthenon sculptures**, brought back from Athens by Lord Elgin. The section on **Assyrian and Babylonian antiquities** is particularly diverse and exhibits the Assyrian palace reliefs of Nineveh. The Far Eastern antiquities, **the Museum of Mankind**, with its statue of Easter Island and the departments devoted to British prehistory archaeology (Lindow man), the Middle Ages (Lewis's 12th century chess set), passing through the Roman era (Portland Valley), are among the highlights of one of the largest museums in the world.

Great Court – Clad with a vast steel-framed canopy by Norman Foster, the square courtyard encloses the circular reading room of the former British Library.

World Conservation and Exhibitions Centre - Bathed in natural light, with a green roof and solar panels, this new centre on the northwest corner is connected to the old buildings by the Great Court. Inaugurated in 2014, it was designed by **Rogers**, Stirk, Harbour + Partners to provide more space and better working conditions for museum researchers, scientists and curators. It also hosts major temporary exhibitions.

RUSSELL SQUARE

E2-3 ⊖ *Russell Square.* Built in 1800, Russell Square is lined with beautiful Victorian homes. The garden, which occupies almost the entire square, gives it a somewhat bucolic air.

CHARLES DICKENS MUSEUM

E2 48 Doughty St. - ⊖ *Russell Square - ☎020 7405 2127 - www. dickensmuseum.com - everyday except Mon 10h-17h (last admission 16h), evening one Thurs a month until 20h - closed 1st Jan and 25 Dec - £9.* The museum occupies the 18th century house in which the most famous British novelist lived with his family from April 1837 to December 1839. It is the only one of his London residences that still exists today.

© Paul Prince/age fotostock

British Museum's Great Court designed by Sir Norman Foster

He only lived there for two years, but it is here that he wrote some of his most important works; *The Adventures of Mr Pickwick*, *Nicholas Nickleby* and *Oliver Twist* in particular. Portraits, furniture, personal effects, manuscripts, the first copies of his novels and the notes he used for his public readings, are set out in different rooms of the house.

King's Cross St Pancras and Camden Town

The opening of the British Library, in 1998, right in the middle of a railway junction (where three of the Capital's six stations concentrate in a radius of 500m!) marked the beginning of the transformation of a zone that for a long time was underprivileged and disreputable. The area, home to the Eurostar at St Pancras International, is still bristled by cranes, but not for much longer. New constructions dedicated to business, culture and nature will soon be all that leaves the ground. Nearby, Camden Town and its markets continue to surf on the «seventies revival» wave to attract its many visitors, especially at the weekend.

▶**Access:** ⊖ Euston Square, King's Cross St Pancras, Camden Town.
Map of Camden Town p. 94. Detachable map D/E1-2.
▶**Tip:** To learn more about the rehabilitation of King's Cross, take advantage of free guided tours organized by King's Cross Visitor Centre *(11 Stable St. - ℘020 3479 1795 - www.kingscross.co.uk).*

BRITISH LIBRARY★★

E1-2 96 Euston Road - ⊖ Euston or King's Cross-St Pancras - ℘019 37 546 060 - www.bl.uk - ♿ - Mon-Thurs 9h30-20h, Fri 9h30-18h, Sat 9h30-17h, Sun & public holidays 11h-17h.
After lengthy and costly construction, the new National Library opened near St Pancras Station in 1998.
The three galleries, belonging to the John Ritblat Gallery, house **Treasures of the British Library**; three millennia of writings from all continents. State of the art technology makes it easy to turn pages with one finger, flipping through rare manuscripts. Among the documents of historical interest are old maps, copies of the **Magna Carta** extorted in 1215 from King John by a legion of nobles, Nelson's last letter and an autograph belonging to Shakespeare (1623).

WELLCOME COLLECTION

D2 183 Euston Road - ⊖ Euston - ℘020 7611 2222 - www.wellcome collection.org - ♿ - Tues-Sat 10h-18h (Thurs 22h), Sun 11h-18h - free - audio guide.
Housed in a large, bright building, the unusual collections belonging to pharmacist and entrepreneur

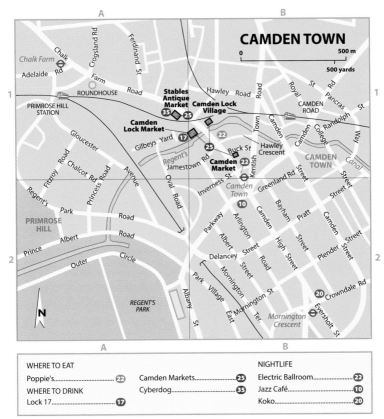

Henry Wellcome (1853-1936) offer an exciting journey through medicine around the world.

ST PANCRAS STATION★

E1 ⊖ *King's Cross-St Pancras.*
It was under the neo-Gothic turrets of the impressive St Pancras Station

(1864) that **Harry Potter**'s departure scenes for Hogwarts were shot, though the series evokes King's Cross station.

KING'S CROSS STATION

E1 ⊖ *King's Cross-St Pancras.*
The big clock at King's Cross station (1852) still commands admiration. It is now the metal structure in the hemicycle of the new **departures hall**, designed by John McAslan + Partners in 2012 which is the subject of all the attention. Fans of the Harry Potter saga can be photographed in front of the famous **9¾ platform** before going to the adjacent shop.

GRANARY SQUARE

E1 ⊖ *King's Cross-St Pancras.*
An iconic hub of the new King's Cross area, this expansive pedestrianized plaza opened in 2012 and extends behind the train station along Regent's Canal. Enjoyed day and night for its **fountain** with a thousand streams of water, it is dominated by an old grain silo, rehabilitated to accommodate the **University of Arts**, plus several shops and restaurants.

SKIP GARDEN

Off map via E1 *Tapper Walk -* ⊖ *King's Cross-St Pancras - www. globalgeneration.org.uk/skip-garden- and-kitchen-1/ Tues-Sat: 10h-16h (restaurant 12h-14h).*
Built using recycled materials partly recovered from nearby yards, this garden is an oasis of creativity. Fresh products served in its charming little restaurant (Moroccan yurt available on rainy days).

CAMDEN TOWN

D1 ⊖ *Camden Town.*
Camden Town was the scene of British rock and pop in the 1990s and is home to residential blocks with large and elegant houses popular with artists, writers and actors. Today, people mostly come to Camden Town for its **flea markets**, the atmosphere and the explosive spectacle of a lively crowd, which mixes punks with colourful mohawks, gothic youth and cool hippies.
At the corner of Camden High Street and Buck Street, **Camden Market** consists of nearly 200 clothes stalls (streetwear, jeans, T-shirts, second-hand clothes, etc.), shoes, jewellery, accessories and junk. Past the bridge over the canal, to your left are the brick buildings of **Camden Lock Market★★**, the first and most famous market in Camden. Set up on the banks of Regent's Canal, it is also the most picturesque, with its craft stalls and exotic cuisine. From there, continue to **Stables Antique Market**, where art shops, second-hand clothes shops and some antique shops fill the stables of the former horse hospital. On the other side of Chalk Farm Road, another general market, **Camden Lock Village**, stretches along the old towpath.

Hampstead★★ *and Highgate*★

At the top of a hill, Hampstead charms with its labyrinth of alleyways and passages, lined with beautiful shops, bars and restaurants. The place also owes its fame to its wooded and hilly landscape, its preserved heath and ponds frequented by bathers in the summer. North of the park, Highgate Village also displays a lot of character with its beautiful houses, cemetery and typical pubs.

▶**Access:** ⊖ Hampstead, Highgate, Archway. Hampstead is north of Regent's Park, and Highgate slightly northeast.
Outside **Detachable** *map.*
▶**Tip:** Visit Hampstead in the morning and, weather permitting, cross the Heath to reach Highgate.

HAMPSTEAD VILLAGE★★

⊖ *Hampstead.* As early as the 18th century, wealthy Londoners owned a country residence in Hampstead. The village also attracted artists, such as John Constable, and writers such as Robert Louis Stevenson, D.H. Lawrence and **John Keats**, whose house you can visit. *(10 Keats Grove - ℘ 020 7332 3868 - www. cityoflondon.gov.uk (tab «Things to do/Keats House») - Wed-Sun 11h-17h - £6.50.*
Flask Walk, which starts off pedestrianized, passes through Gardnor House (1736), decorated at the rear with a full length bay window, and ends in New End Square.

FENTON HOUSE★★

*Hampstead Grove, NW3 6SP -
⊖ Hampstead - ℘020 7435 3471 -
www.nationaltrust.org.uk - ﬔ -*

Mar-Oct: Wed-Sun and p. holidays 11h-17h, closed rest of year - £7.70. Wrought iron gates, designed by **Tijou** (1707), open onto a red brick house (1693), the oldest and largest in Hampstead. You will discover the magnificent Benton-Fletcher collection of **18 keyboard instruments**, in particular, made between 1540 and 1805, plus a beautiful garden.

HAMPSTEAD HEATH★★

⊖ *Belsize Park.* This is one of the rare examples of urban heathland. The site is a very popular place for walking and entertainment (big fairs on Easter Mon., summer and spring holidays). Three ponds and a swimming pool are open for swimming.

© SuperStock/age fotostock

Kenwood House, Hampstead Heath

KENWOOD HOUSE ★★

Hampstead Lane, NW3 7JR - ⊖ Archway, Golders Green then bus 210 - ☏020 8348 1286 - www. english-heritage.org.uk - ♿ - 10h-17h (Feb-Mar 16h), park 8h-sunset - closed 1st Jan and 24-26 Dec - free - restaurant.

Stucco white, the castle reigns over harmonious nature. Its elegant architecture inspired by antiquity reflects the Adam style.

Note the **Adam Library★★** designed as a reception room, and the beautiful **collection of paintings★★**.

In the dining room; **Rembrandt**'s *late self-portrait*, *Pieter van den Broecke* by **Frans Hals**, **Vermeer**'s *The Guitar Player*, in the small room; *Marines* by

Van de Velde and a **Turner**. On the landing and in the breakfast room, canvases of an unusual character by Gainsborough (T*he Market Cart, Two Shepherd Boys with Dogs Fighting*). On the first floor, a beautiful series of portraits from **the Suffolk collection**.

HIGHGATE ★

⊖ *Archway, Highgate.*

A 16th century green hill, Highgate attracted rich merchants from the 17th century who built summer houses there. Outside the modern constructions, the village centred on Pond Square and High Street has kept a country feel.

HIGHGATE CEMETERY ★★

Swain's Lane, N6 6PJ - ⊖ Archway - ☏020 8340 1834 - highgatecemetery. org - East Cemetery: Mon-Fri 10h-17h, w/end 11h-17h (£4); guided tour Sat at 14h (£8) - West Cemetery: guided tour only (1hr) Mon-Fri 13h45, w/end 11h-16h (£12, including entry to East Cemetery) - various events: conferences, concerts (prog. on website).

Surrounded by mystery, this cemetery, in service since 1839, is home to some 53,000 graves of unknown and known people, such as the scholar **George Eliot** (1819-1880) and **Karl Marx** (1818-1883), whose energetic bust was carved in 1956 by Laurence Bradshaw. The western part contains some remarkable funerary monuments, as well as the tombs of **Michael Faraday** (1791-1867) and the painter **Dante Gabriel Rossetti** (1828-1882).

The East End

It is here that you will discover a cosmopolitan and authentic London, more than in Notting Hill or Camden. When in the early 1990s, penniless artists sniffed out London's East End, attracted by the vast moderately priced spaces, they did not imagine that the rumour of a new El Dorado would spread like wildfire. Since then, a multitude of galleries, bars, restaurants and trendy clubs have blossomed. Nevertheless, the East End, a traditional land of immigration, retains a vibrant cultural diversity.

▶ **Access:** ⊖ Liverpool Street, Aldgate East, Shoreditch High Street (Overground), Old Street.
***Map of the area** p. 98-99. **Detachable map** H1-2-3.*
▶ **Tip:** Visit the area on Sundays to take advantage of the markets. Begin with Columbia Road flower market (ideally early in the morning to avoid the crowd), go down to Brick Lane market, followed by Sunday Upmarket and finishing with Spitalfields Market.

© Bombaert/iStockphoto.com

Brick Lane and The Old Truman's Brewery

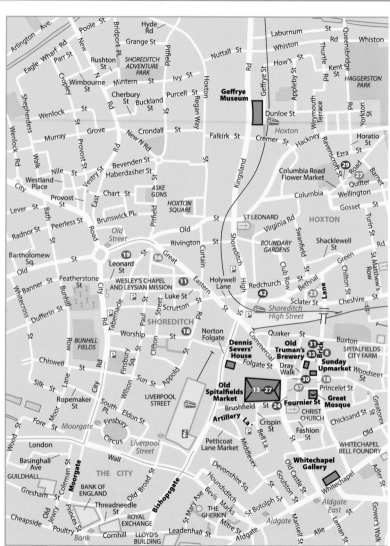

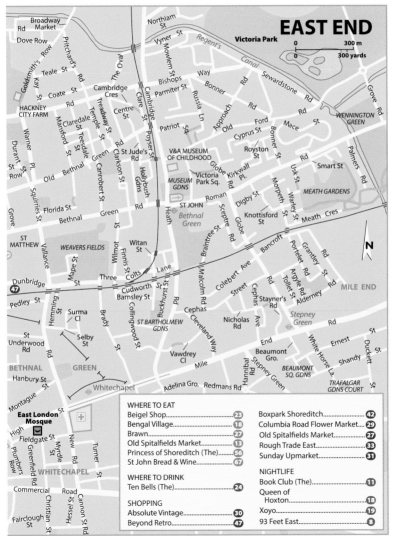

EAST END

WHERE TO EAT

Beigel Shop	**23**
Bengal Village	**18**
Brawn	**27**
Old Spitalfields Market	**13**
Princess of Shoreditch (The)	**56**
St John Bread & Wine	**67**

WHERE TO DRINK

Ten Bells (The)	**24**

SHOPPING

Absolute Vintage	**30**
Beyond Retro	**47**
Boxpark Shoreditch	**42**
Columbia Road Flower Market	**29**
Old Spitalfields Market	**27**
Rough Trade East	**33**
Sunday Upmarket	**31**

NIGHTLIFE

Book Club (The)	**11**
Queen of Hoxton	**18**
Xoyo	**19**
93 Feet East	**8**

SPITALFIELDS

H3 ⊖ *Liverpool Street.*
A former historic textile industry area, Spitalfields today marks the border between the City and the East End, with its large indoor market. Lively and mixed, it is full of galleries, shops, underground clubs and street art.

Old Spitalfields Market★

The old market was founded in 1862 but, in 1991, the largest of London's merchandise depots was moved to Leyton, and Spitalfields Market was transformed into a hotchpotch of temporary stalls and ethnic restaurants. Today, this component remains in the eastern part under a Victorian arch (1892), which runs along Commercial Street. On the west, the City side, a large part of the market was destroyed to make room for a **Norman Foster** project combining office buildings and a shopping centre.
♿ *Addresses /Where to Eat p. 114 and Shopping p. 132.*

Artillery Lane

It is one of the narrowest and oldest streets in the area. A typical house is located at No. 9 Artillery Passage.

Dennis Severs' House

18 Folgate St. - ⊖ Liverpool Street or Shoreditch High Street (Overground) - ☏020 7247 4013 - www.dennissevers house.co.uk - guided tour (45 mins): Mon 12h-14h, Sun 12h-16h (£10); candlelight tour (45 mins - on reservation): Mon, Wed & Fri 17h-21h (£15).
Restored, or rather staged, the Georgian house belonging to **Dennis Severs**, an American artist who died in 1999, tells a story from the beginning of the 20th century. Odours and soundscapes contribute to total immersion, further accentuated by a candlelit visit.

Fournier Street

The street includes beautiful Georgian houses (1718-1728), once occupied by silk manufacturers.

Old Truman's Brewery

The building named Truman is recognizable by its large brick chimney. A former 18th century brewery, it extends on both sides of Brick Lane and now houses bars, shops, offices, as well as the **Sunday**

© Y. Kanazawa/Michelin

Old Spitalfields Market

Upmarket (♿ *p.140*). In the courtyard, impressive installations, including a giant Space Invader, enhance the industrial setting.

Brick Lane★

The Long street area of Brick Lane hosts a large Bangladeshi community. An endearing and lively artery on Sundays, you must walk in both directions. On one side, there are fabric shops (witness to the strong textile tradition), ironmongers and barbers; on the other, tandoori restaurants.

The history of the **mosque**, which was first a chapel and then a synagogue, reflects the different waves of immigration that populated the area. Its contemporary minaret (2010) now serves as a landmark.

On Sunday morning, a **flea market** occupies the surroundings of Bethnal Green Road, Sclater and Cheshire Street.

WHITECHAPEL

Whitechapel Gallery★

H3 *77-82 Whitechapel High St. - ⊖ Aldgate East - ☎020 7522 7888 - www.whitechapelgallery.org - ♿ - Tues-Sun 11h-18h (Thurs 21h) - free, except the big annual exhibition-cafe, bookstore.*

Inaugurated in 1901 in the Arts & Crafts style, the gallery welcomed future masters of modern art such as Picasso, Pollock, Rothko and Frida Kahlo, as well as contemporary artists **David Hockney** and Gilbert & George while they were unknown.

SHOREDITCH AND HOXTON

H1-2 ⊖ *Old Street, Hoxton (Overground).*

Ordinary before becoming trendy, invested in by artists and enjoyed by night owls, Shoreditch and Hoxton are gradually being gentrifying to make way for the fashionable *Made in Bio* and yuppie brands. Rivington Street, Redchurch Street or Chance Street are still decorated with stencils, graffiti and street art stickers.

Geffrye Museum★

136 Kingsland Rd - ⊖ Old Street or Hoxton (Overground) - ☎020 7739 9893 - www.geffrye-museum.org.uk - ♿ - Tues-Sun and public holidays including Mon 10h-17h - closed 1st Jan, Fri saint and 24-26 Dec - free, except temporary exhibitions - audio guide (£3.50) - gardens (Apr-Oct) café.

This museum illustrates daily life of the British 16th to 20th century middle class, through the reconstruction of interiors. In addition to the herb garden, other plots have also been developed according to the design at different periods.

Docklands★

The landscape undergoes a radical change at the point where the Thames creates a long loop, facing Greenwich, between Tower Pier and the Thames Barrier. The most brilliant element is certainly Canary Wharf, which eclipses the other sites of interest. It is recommended you go there by Docklands Light Railway. The impression of entering a futuristic city reveals the extent of redevelopment of the docks, a sign of the continued extension of London to the east.

▶**Access:** ⊖ Tower Hill, Canary Wharf, Canary Wharf (DLR), West Shadwell (DLR), West India Quay (DLR).
Map of the area p. 104-105. **Outside Detachable** map.
▶**Tip:** It's best to visit the Docklands in the week as it's deserted at the weekend.

ST KATHARINE'S DOCKS★

⊖ *Tower Hill.* Located just a stone's throw from the Tower of London (⦿*p.58*), this pleasant **marina** lined with offices, shops, restaurants and luxury flats replaced the docks in 1968 that had occupied the site since 1828. There is nothing left of the St. Katharine by the Tower hospice which gave its name to the place. Founded in 1148, it welcomed refugees from Europe, but the land was bought in 1825 by St Katharine's Dock Company who built two basins and warehouses. Terraces allow you to enjoy the setting, which is very pleasant on sunny days.

MUSEUM OF LONDON DOCKLANDS★★

West India Quay - ⊖ *West India Quay (DLR) - ☎020 7001 9844 - www.museumoflondon.org.uk/ docklands -* ♿ *- 10h-18h (last*

admission 17h40) - closed 24-26 Dec - free except exhibitions - guided tour (75 mins), check the timetable on the website.
A visit to this fascinating museum, located at No.1 Warehouse, provides an insight into the importance of the Thames in its development of London and the history of Docklands.
On two levels, it celebrates the influence of port activities on the social and economic life of the city, from the Roman period to the present day. We thus discover the complex operation of the docks in the great maritime commerce era. Animations show the flow of ships returning to port, directed, according to their origin, towards specific basins. The exhibition looks at the diverse nature of goods arriving from all parts of the globe. Docklands is also a needy population of workers, Dockers, families with difficult living conditions and whose demands have been at the root of many social conflicts and

strikes. The reconstruction of a set of dark alleys, with their taverns, shops and miserable homes helps us to perceive this reality.

ISLE OF DOGS★

⊖ West India Quay (DLR) or Canary Wharf (DLR).
This tongue of land nestled in a meander of the Thames is called the Isle of Dogs, the kennels established in the 16th century by King Henry VIII. It was then covered with swampy grasslands, where cattle grazed.
At the beginning of the 19th century, the creation of the **West India Docks** would very quickly transform the sector. A populous neighbourhood developed around three basins in the north in 1802 and 1806, and its main wharf, Canary Wharf.
After the closure of the docks in the 1980s, the Isle of Dogs was the subject of a project in East London to develop an «annex» to the City. A restored Canary Wharf has experienced a success that was not expected.

CANARY WHARF★

⊖ Canary Wharf (DLR).
The renaissance of Canary Wharf, which in less than two decades has become a 1st class business district, began in 1988 with the construction of new skyscrapers around Cabot Square, including **One Canada Square** and **Canary Wharf Tower** (235m). Designed by the Argentinian architect Cesar Pelli, this 50 storey stainless steel clad obelisk tower, reflects the light, standing out like a lighthouse. Fully funded by private funds, Canary Wharf has since attracted the establishment of several prestigious firms and banks, as well as media groups. More recently, Canary Wharf has sought to establish itself as a major shopping centre with the creation of Cabot Place and Jubilee Place, large shopping centres with more than 200 shops.

THE O2

Peninsula Square - ⊖ North Greenwich, Royal Victoria (DLR), then Emirates Air Line cable car (www. emiratesairline.co.uk, One Way £4.50). Access possible with the Thames Clippers River Bus from the Coca-Cola London Eye - ℘020 8463 2000 - www.theo2.co.uk - ♿ - 9h-1h - free, except activities.
Situated on the south bank of the Thames' meander on the peninsula of Greenwich, the former Millennium Dome built by **Richard Rogers** forms a vast fabric structure in fibreglass, 365m in diameter and 50m high, it is supported by 12 steel masts, equivalent to 10 x the volume of St. Paul's Cathedral. It was reconverted to a leisure complex including shops, restaurants, bars, nightclubs, cinema multiplexes, ten pin bowling and several concert halls, one of which has a 20,000 seating capacity (O2 Arena).

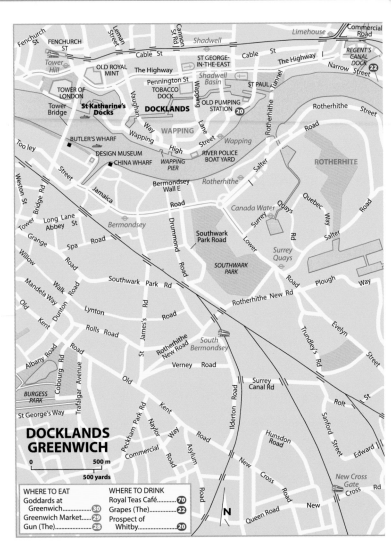

Fenchurch St

FENCHURCH ST

Leman Street

Cannon St Rd

Shadwell

Limehouse

Commercial Road

Tower Hill

OLD ROYAL MINT

Cable St

ST GEORGE-IN-THE-EAST

Cable St

The Highway

REGENT'S CANAL DOCK

22

Narrow Street

The Highway

Pennington St

Shadwell Basin

TOWER OF LONDON

TOBACCO DOCK

Wapping

ST PAUL's

Tunnel

Rotherhithe

Rotherhithe Street

Tower Bridge

St Katharine's Docks

DOCKLANDS

OLD PUMPING STATION

20

Rotherhithe Road

Wapping Way

WAPPING

Lane

Too ley Street

BUTLER'S WHARF

Wapping

High Street

Wapping

ROTHERHITE

Weston St

DESIGN MUSEUM

CHINA WHARF

WAPPING PIER

RIVER POLICE BOAT YARD

Salter Road

Bermondsey Wall E

Rotherhithe

Quebec Way

Road

Tower Bridge Rd

Jamaica Road

Canada Water

Surrey Quays

Salter Rd

Long Lane

Abbey St

Bermondsey

Drummond Road

Southwark Park Road

Rd

Grange Road

Spa Road

Lower

Surrey Quays

Willow

SOUTHWARK PARK

104

Mandela Way

Walk

Dunton Road

Southwark Park Rd

James's Rd

Rotherhithe New Rd

Plough Way

Old Kent Road

Lynton

Road

Rolls Road

Rotherhithe New Road

South Bermondsey

Road

Evelyn

Trundley's Rd

Street

Albany Road

Cobourg Rd

Trafalgar Avenue

Verney Road

Surrey Canal Rd

Rolt St

BURGESS PARK

St George's Way

Old

Kent

Naylor

Way

Road

Ilderton Road

Hunsdon Road

Sanford Street

Edward

DOCKLANDS GREENWICH

Peckham Park Rd

Commercial

Asylum Road

New Cross Road

New Cross Gate

Cross Rd

0   500 m

500 yards

Road

Queen Road

New

N

ST ANNE
Upper N St
RICHARD GREEN'S STATUE
E India Dock Rd
FINANCIAL TIMES BUILDING
Silvertown Way
W India Dock Road
E India Dock Rd
BLACKWALL
Lower Lea Crossing
DOCKMASTER'S HOUSE
Museum of London Docklands
Cotton St
EAST INDIA DOCKS
CANNON WORKSHOPS
Aspen
The New Blackwall Tunnel
Cabot Place
Canary Wharf Tower
NEW BILLINGSGATE MARKET
Blackwall Tunnel
The O₂
Emirates Air Line
EMIRATES ROYAL DOCKS
CANARY WHARF
WEST INDIA DOCKS
Canary Wharf
Preston's
N
Olympian
EMIRATES GREENWICH PENINSULA
JUBILEE PARK
Jubilee Place
28
North Greenwich
Marsh
Wall
Blue Bridge
Edmund Halley Way
East Parkside
Westferry
Marsh
Wall
ISLAND HISTORY TRUST
Meridian
Millennium Way
West
Parkside
DOCKLANDS
Manchester
Road
Greenwich
Blackwall Tunnel Southern Approach
Bugsby's Way
Road
Isle of Dogs
MILLWALL DOCKS
E Ferry Road
Olympian Way
MUDCHUTE PARK & FARM
Spindrift Ave.
MILLWALL PARK
CHRIST CHURCH
Lane
Tunnel Avenue
Westferry
Manchester
Road
Road
Ballast Quay
Barning St
21
Woolwich Rd
Thames
Road
ISLAND GARDENS
TRINITY HOSPITAL
Trafalgar Rd
Blackwall
Grove St
Greenwich Footway Tunnel
GREENWICH PIER
Old Royal Naval College
Humber Road
DEPTFORD
Cutty Sark
CHAPEL
ST NICHOLAS
GREENWICH
GREENWICH GATEWAY VISITOR CENTRE
PAINTED HALL
Coleraine Rd
Creek
Deptford
Road
29
Queen's House
Mare
Norman Rd
St Alfege
30
National Maritime Museum
Westcombe Park Rd
Deptford High
Greenwich DLR
Greenwich Market
Flamsteed House
Peter Harrison Planetarium
Vanbrugh Hill
St
High St
Fan Museum
The Avenue
Royal Observatory Greenwich
Way
New Cross Rd
70
Hyde Vale
Crooms Hill
General Wolfe Rd
Greenwich Park
Greenwich S St
Blackheath Ave
Lewisham Way
Brookmill Road
Blackheath
Hill
Ranger's House
Charlton
Shooters Hill Road

105

Greenwich★★★

Located on the south bank of the Thames, facing Docklands, the name of this area of London, is known around the world for its meridian. Greenwich however cannot be summed up solely for this imaginary line, or even the observatory where the first research on the calculation of longitude was conducted. This former royal residence boasts a rich historical past and remarkable architecture that earned it UNESCO World Heritage status. Its royal park, the biggest in London, and the banks of the river are both pleasant places to walk to escape the suffocating heat of the capital in the summer.

▶**Access:** ⊖ Cutty Sark (DLR). Greenwich is on the south bank of the Thames, opposite the Isle of Dogs. A pedestrian tunnel (Greenwich Footway Tunnel) connects the two areas. Access by boat with the River Bus Service from Embankment or Tower Bridge (RB1: www.tfl.gov.uk).
***Map of area** p. 104-105. Outside **Detachable** map*
▶**Tip:** Avoid the particularly busy weekend.

Cutty Sark

© _ultraforma_/iStockphoto.com

GREENWICH MARKET

www.greenwichmarketlondon.com - 9h30-17h30.
Located a short walk from Cutty Sark DLR station, this charming indoor market contributes to the «village» atmosphere of Greenwich. Installed in 1700, it includes pretty shops, cafes and stalls selling art, craft, food and a flea market (*Tues, Thurs and Fri*). For a pleasant stroll or a quick lunch.

CUTTY SARK★★

King William Walk - ☎020 8858 4422 - www.rmg.co.uk - ♿ - 10h-17h (last admission 16h15) - closed 24-26 Dec - £13.50; possibility of ticket combined with other attractions such as the Royal Observatory.
Brought in 1869 from Dumbarton

Old Royal Naval Collage

shipyards in Scotland, this majestic three master was intended for the import of tea from China. It quickly became famous because of its speed; its best distance in one day was 580km, with its 10,000m2 of sails fully deployed. After the opening of the Suez Canal, *Cutty Sark* competing with steamboats, transported wool from Australia. It took 70 days to get there. On the way back it took 80 days with a full load (5,000 wool balls) to complete the perilous journey including the crossing of Cape Horn. Sold to a Portuguese company in 1895, the ship returned to England in 1922 and was converted into a training ship before being transferred to Greenwich in 1954, put in a dry dock and turned into a nautical museum. Severely damaged by a fire in 2007, it was restored and reopened to the public in 2012.

OLD ROYAL NAVAL COLLEGE ★★

King William Walk - ☏020 8269 4747 - www.ornc.org - 8h-23h; Painted Hall and chapel: 10h-17h; check the calendar online as the place is often closed due to private functions - closed 24-26 Dec - free - (possibility of guided tour (info. at the Visitor Centre).

The college accommodates the University of Greenwich campus. King Charles' Pavilion is occupied by Trinity College of Music and the buildings overlooking the Thames are home to a naval school

NATIONAL MARITIME MUSEUM★★

Romney Rd - ☏020 8312 6565 - www.rmg.co.uk - ⚹ - 10h-17h (last admission 16h30) - closed 24-26 Dec - free (except temporary exhibitions).
The National Maritime Museum's collections illustrate Great Britain's naval history. Particular emphasis is placed on commercial development with the triangular trade and the East India Company, but also on Admiral Nelson. The visitor's attention is also drawn to the consequences of modern progress on marine life. Many activities are aimed at children who will enjoy themselves.

QUEEN'S HOUSE★★

☏020 8858 4422 - www.rmg.co.uk - 10h-17h (last admission 16h30) - closed 24-26 Dec - free (except temp. exhibitions).
This elegant villa, which holds temporary exhibitions, distinguishes itself by its white colour, its beautiful iron horseshoe shaped staircase descending from the terrace on the north facade and its loggia on the south side, in front of the park.

ST ALFEGE

Greenwich Church St. - ☏020 8853 0687 - st-alfege.org - Mon-Fri 11h-16h, Sat 10h-16h, Sun 12h-16h - brochure, concert programme.
This early church witnessed the baptism of **Henry VIII**. It was erected on the site of the martyr of Alfege,

Archbishop of Canterbury killed by the Danes in 1012.

FAN MUSEUM★

12 Crooms Hill - ☏020 8305 1441 - www.thefanmuseum.org.uk - ⚹ - Tues-Sat 11h-17h, Sun 12h-17h - fan making workshop (3 hrs) on request: 1st Sun of the month at 14h (£25) - closed 1st Jan and 24-26 Dec - £4 - audio guide - brochure.
This magnificent museum has some 2,000 **fans**. Permanent exhibitions explore the subject; methods and materials of manufacture, types, origins. Temporary exhibitions are organized according to the themes of inspiration of their decoration.

GREENWICH PARK

Surrounded by a fence in 1433 and enclosed by a wall under the Stuarts, the park is the oldest enclosed royal estate. On about 90 Ha, its avenues of sweet chestnut trees and vast lawns ascend towards a 52 metre high hill over the Thames, and is crowned by the former Royal Observatory and General Wolfe's monument. You can take advantage of a very beautiful **view** of London here.

ROYAL OBSERVATORY GREENWICH★★

Blackheath Ave. - ☏020 8858 4422 - www.rmg.co.uk - ⚹ - 10h-17h (last admission 16h30) - closed 24-26 Dec - Astronomy Centre: free; Meridian Courtyard and Flamsteed House:

£9.50; planetarium: £7.50; combined ticket: £12.50; poss. of ticket combined with the Cutty Sark *- brochure.*

In 1675, Charles II asked **Christopher Wren** to «*build a small observatory in our Greenwich Park to find the longitude of places to perfect navigation and astronomy*» Wren, a former astronomer, built a red brick house, topped with a balustrade and with small panelled domes «to *serve as a dwelling for the astronomer and add a particular pump*» At the top of one of them, a red ball put in place in 1833 slips abruptly along a mast at 13:00 sharp (GMT time), allowing sailors on the Thames to set their watch.

The visit begins in the Meridian Courtyard, where **Greenwich Meridian**, at zero longitude, is represented by a copper rail.

You will then discover **Flamsteed House**, named after the Royal Astronomer John Flamsteed who lived there. The nicely proportioned **Octagon Room**, with a high ceiling, has been restored and refurbished to its original state. Another presentation, using the most recent interactive multimedia tools, traces the history of calculating latitude and longitude.

Peter Harrison Planetarium – Schedules vary according to the projections. Some sessions are prohibited for children -5 years (consult the website). Built in a cone shape, it includes 250 bronze plates welded and polished to give the impression of only forming one.

The north side of the cone is aligned with the zenith (point perpendicular to the horizon perceived from Greenwich). The south side points to the North Star. The angle of the slope (51° 28' 44") is equal to the latitude of the Royal Observatory.

RANGER'S HOUSE★

Chesterfield Walk, Greenwich Park - ☎020 8853 0035 - www. english-heritage.org.uk - ♿ - guided tour only (1h30, max. 25 pers.) - Apr-Jun): Sun-Wed: 11h & 14h; Jul-Sept: Sun-Wed: 11h-17h - closed rest of the year - £8.20.

This house was originally a small brick villa. Rounded wings were added by Philip Stanhope, Count Chesterfield (1694-1773), politician, diplomat and man of wit. The south gallery was then built. 25m long, it is decorated with a panelled ceiling and lit by three bow windows whose satisfied owner, said: «*All three different, and the best perspectives of the world*». The gardens have retained all their beauty. The panelled rooms on the ground and first floors house **Wernher's European art collection**, magnificent and reflecting the eclectic taste of **Sir Julius Wernher** (1850-1912), a philanthropist and mining magnate. This collection brings together some rare religious paintings by Filippo Lippi and paintings by Dutch masters (Van Ostade, de Hooch), as well as Renaissance jewellery and bronzes.

Quick getaways

Here are some ideas for day trips, easily accessible from the centre of London and ideal for escaping to the countryside in fine weather. If it's raining, you can still opt to visit the Making of Harry Potter at Warner Bros. Studios. Tip from the apprentice wizards is to meet on platform 9³/⁴ !

▶ **Tip:** For more details, refer to the MICHELIN London Green Guide

RICHMOND

⊖ *Richmond. The town is found south west of London, between the A3 and the M3. Accessible by boat with Thames River Boats (www.wpsa. co.uk - Apr-Oct).*

Bordering the River Thames, Richmond enjoys a country atmosphere thanks to its green parks and golf courses. The small town is very popular for its historic pubs, good restaurants, antique shops and chic shops.

Richmond Palace, one of the Tudors' favourite residences, and other beautiful homes are reminiscent of an aristocratic past.

⊗ **Do not miss**: Richmond Park with its views and free roaming deer, as well as a walk along the Thames.

WARNER BROS. STUDIOS- BEHIND THE SCENES OF HARRY POTTER

Leavesden is 20 miles northwest of London and accessible by the A41 and A405. By train: 20 mins from Euston Station (stop Watford Junction), then 15 mins by bus. By bus: shuttle (1hr 15) departs from Victoria station or Baker Street.

In the former hangers of the Rolls Royce factory on the Leavesden aerodrome, Warner Bros. studios welcome Harry Potter fans into a space of 14000 m².

It's here, for ten years, that Daniel Radcliffe (Harry), Rupert Grint (Ron) and Emma Watson (Hermione) have been shooting the eight films adapted from the literary saga devoted to the little sorcerer.

☏0845 084 0900 - www. wbstudiotour.co.uk - £37 (child £29).

⊗ **Do not miss**: the Hogwarts Castle model in the Model Room.

KEW GARDENS ★★★

⊖ *Kew Gardens. To the southwest of London via the A4 and A315. By boat: with Thames River Boats (www.wpsa. co.uk - Apr-Oct).*

The Thames describes a long loop around Kew, a residential area with a village atmosphere. In good weather it is delightful to visit the Royal Botanical Gardens, bordered on the north by the river, to discover rare species, large greenhouses and pretty valleys. A footbridge 20m from the ground allows you to discover a part of the garden from a different perspective and to observe the birds more closely.

☏020 83325655 - www.kew.org - £15.50 (£2.50).

♿ **Do not miss:** Kew Palace: the palm treehouse, the bamboo garden, the view of London from the top of the pagoda.

HAMPTON COURT★★★

23km south west of London, via the A308 and A309. By train: 30 minutes from Waterloo Station (Hampton Court stop). By boat: from Westminster or Richmond (Apr-Sept) with Thames River Boats (www.wpsa. co.uk) or Turks (www.turks.co.uk). Located in a romantic setting on the banks of the Thames, Henry VIII's favourite royal palace has been an ideal retreat for many rulers. These glorious buildings and gardens that illustrate all kinds of styles, testify to the royal power and its wealth.

☏0844 482 7777 - www.hrp.org.uk - £23 (child £11.50).

♿ **Do not miss:** the kitchens, the large flats, the maze.

WINDSOR CASTLE★★★

36 km west of London via the M4 (exit junction 6). By train: 50 mins from Waterloo Station (stop Windsor Central); the castle is less than 15 mins walk from the station. By bus: from Victoria Station, bus No. 701 or 702 with Green Line Bus (www.greenline. co.uk).

© www.visitlondon.com

Palm House, Kew Gardens

Perched on a steep cliff in the middle of a beautiful park, Windsor Castle's turrets overlook a charming little town nestled in the Thames Valley. Windsor is an exciting example of the transformation of a medieval castle into a sumptuous royal residence. Its monarchical position gives the city a lot of character. Also worthy of interest on the other side of the bridge are Eton College's buildings *(www.etoncollege.com).* ☏0303 123 7334 - www.royalcollection.org.uk - £20.50 (child £12).

♿ **Do not miss:** the State Apartments, St George's Chapel.

Addresses

113

Marylebone High Street
© Pawel Libera/www.visitlondon.com

🍴

Where to eat

At lunchtime, there are options to suit all budgets. You can eat on the go without spending a fortune, with various cafes, pubs and coffee shops offering low-cost options such as sandwiches, salads, bagels, soups, jacket potatoes etc. Also try exploring the many and varied food markets, and street food stalls and vans, dotted around the city, which offer exciting and inexpensive world food dishes. There are many other interesting restaurant and cafe options housed inside the capital's museums and galleries, or head to food retailers such as Marks & Spencer, Waitrose, Sainsbury's or Tesco for a wide range of ready-prepared sandwiches. For dinner, indulge yourself – London has become a centre for gastronomy, offering high-end food in beautifully designed surroundings, with dishes of all cuisines and styles offering a feast for the eyes and the palette.

The price ranges mentioned below, correct at the time of going to press, are for a complete meal excluding drinks. ♿ *Eating out p. 154 and London specialities p. 183.*

♿ Find the addresses on our plans with numbered pads (ex. ❶). The coordinates in red (eg C2) refer to the detachable plane.

TRAFALGAR SQUARE

Local map p. 17

Under £15 (19 €)

㉖ **Café in the Crypt** – *E4 - St Martin-in-the-Fields - Duncannon St. - ⊖ Charing Cross - ☎020 7766 1158 - www.stmartin-in-the-fields.org - ♿ - Mon-Tues, 8am-8pm; Wed 8:30pm, Thur-Sat -9pm; Sun 6pm - Closed 25 Dec.* This subterraneous, self-service café is housed in the vaulted crypt of St. Martin's in-the-Fields. Tasty, wholesome food is served up in atmospheric surroundings. Jazz concerts on Wednesday evenings (reservations required after 7pm).

From £20 to £35 (25 to 45 €)

㊶ **The National Dining Rooms** – *E4 - Trafalgar Sq. - ⊖ Charing Cross or Leicester Square - ☎020 7747 2525 - www.peytonandbyrne. co.uk - Sat-Thur, 10am-5pm , Fri 10am-8pm - Closed 24-26 Dec and 1 Jan.* Designed by famous architect David Collins, this restaurant sits above the National Gallery. The classic menu includes traditional British dishes and afternoon tea (3pm).

ST JAMES'S

Local map p. 25

From £15 to £30 (19 to 38 €)

❶ **Inn the Park** – *D5 - St James's Park - ⊖ Charing Cross or Westminster - ☎020 7451 9999 - www.innthepark.com - ♿ - Mon-Fri,*

8am-9pm; Sat, 9am-9pm; Sun, 9am-4:30pm. In the heart of St James's Park, this is the ideal spot for a meal before going to watch the changing of the guard at Buckingham Palace. Breakfast includes English breakfast, pancakes and toast, followed by lunches made with quality, seasonal produce. Sit on the terrace on the roof in fine weather.

15 **Yoshino** – *D4* - *3 Piccadilly Pl. - ⊖ Piccadilly Circus - ℘020 7287 6622 - www.yoshino.net - ᵫ - Mon-Fri, 12pm-3pm and 5:30pm-11pm, Sat 12pm-11pm - closed Sun.* Just a few steps from the bustle of Piccadilly, the minimalist setting of this Japanese restaurant offers a calm haven away from the crowds. The lunch box, accompanied by a matcha tea, is a delicious and nutritious option.

From £25 to £40 (32 to 51 €)

63 **Gymkhana** – *D4* - *42 Albemarle St. - ⊖ Green Park - ℘020 3011 5900 - www.gymkhanalondon.com - ᵫ - Mon-Sat, 12pm -2:30pm, 5:30pm-10:30pm - Closed Sun.* From the ceiling fans and carved woodwork, to the copper percolators and traditional cutlery, everything breathes the cosy atmosphere of a colonial gentlemen's club. Indian cuisine with European influences, using the best local produce, including game. Deer biryani confit with saffron is a highlight.

From £30 to 55 (38 to 70 €)

47 **Quaglino's** – *D4* - *16 Bury St. - ⊖ Green Park - ℘020 7930 6767 - www.quaglinos-restaurant.co.uk - ᵫ - Mon-Thur 12pm-3pm, 5:30pm-1am, Fri-Sat 12pm-3pm,* *5:30pm-3am - bar ouv. tte la journée.* This brasserie, where you can watch the chefs in the open kitchen, is very popular, with a loyal, well-heeled following. Seasonal menus change through the year. Booking essential.

MAYFAIR AND PICCADILLY

Local map p. 28-29

Under £15 (19 €)

32 **Tibits** – *D4* - *12-14 Heddon St. - ⊖ Piccadilly Circus - ℘020 7758 4110 - www.tibits.co.uk - Mon-Wed 9am-10:30pm, Thur-Sat 9am-12am Sun 11:30am-10:30pm.* Set just back from Regent Street on a small road lined with upscale bars and restaurants. The vegetarian buffet is recommended – food is priced fairly and customers pay by weight. In summer there is a terrace with large communal tables.

From £30 to £50 (38 to 64 €)

57 **Scott's** – *C4* - *20 Mount St. - ⊖ Bond Street - ℘020 7495 7309 - www.scotts-restaurant.com - 12pm-10:30pm, Sun 12pm-10pm.* If you like fish and seafood, this is the place to go. The decor, the food and the service are all refined. A sophisticated atmosphere and good wine list.

SOHO

Local map p. 28-29

Under £15 (19 €)

62 **Golden Union** – *D3* - *38 Poland St. - ⊖ Oxford Circus - ℘020 7434 1933 - www.goldenunion.co.uk - ᵫ - Mon-Sat 11:30am-10pm, Sun*

115

11:30am-6pm. A safe bet for fish and chips, to be eaten on the spot or taken away. Generous portions, fresh fish, crispy fries that aren't too oily and a good atmosphere.

64 Koya Bar – *D4* - *50 Frith St. - ⊖ Leicester Square or Tottenham Court Road - www.koya.co.uk - Mon-Fri 8:30am-10:30pm, Thur-Fri 8:30am-11pm, Sat 9:30am-11pm, Sun 9:30am-10pm.* In the heart of busy Soho there is a Zen atmosphere in this little bar. Udon noodles are served in broth, cold or hot, with lots of different accompaniments. Perfect for a healthy and quick lunch.

From £15 to £35 (€ 19 to € 45)

2 BAO – *D4* - *53 Lexington St. - ⊖ Oxford Circus or Piccadilly Circus - www.baolondon.com - Mon-Sat 12pm-3pm, 5:30pm-10pm.* Taiwanese, filled, steamed, dough buns (bao) are the speciality here. The signature version comes with braised pork, coriander and peanut powder, with chicken and lamb also available. Accompany the small buns with a peanut milk or smoked tea. This spot is very popular and there are often queues down the street, so arrive a little before opening to avoid the busiest times. Other address in Fitzrovia, 31 Windmill St.

3 Baiwei – *E4* - *8 Little Newport St. - ⊖ Leicester Square - ☎020 7494 3605 - 12pm-9:30pm.* It isn't easy to choose between the many venues in China Town, but if you like spice, then restaurants specialising in Sichuan cuisine are a good choice. On the fiery and varied menu at Baiwei (which translates as 'one hundred flavours')

BAO Soho

© BAO Soho

are the likes of catfish with chillis, gong bao tofu and pickled beans.

25 Busaba Eathai – *D4* - *106-110 Wardour St. - ⊖ Oxford Circus - ☎020 7255 8686 - www.busaba.com - 12pm-11pm, Fri-Sat 12pm-11:30pm, Sun 12pm-10pm - Closed 25 Dec.* Modern Thai cuisine served on large communal tables in relaxed surroundings. Crunchy vegetable salads, stir fries and curries, all scented and perfectly spiced. Budget-friendly.

14 10 Greek Street – *D4* - *10 Greek St. - ⊖ Tottenham Court Road - ☎020 7734 4677 - www.10greekstreet.com - Mon-Sat 12pm-2:30pm, 5:30pm-10.45pm - Closed Sun.* This unpretentious neighbourhood bistro attracts customers from far and wide and offers good value for money. The short, modern menu changes daily with inventive, seasonal dishes.

53 **Yauatcha Soho** – *D4* - *15-17 Broadwick St. -* ⊖ *Piccadilly Circus - ℘020 7494 8888 - www.yauatcha. com/soho - Sun-Thur 12pm-10pm, Fri-Sat 12pm-10:30pm - Closed 25 Dec.* A stylish Chinese restaurant in Soho, with a very contemporary interior (bright aquarium and stone walls) by Christian Liaigre. Specialities include dim sum and other, fragrant small plates. The exquisite desserts and pastries are a must-try.

From £20 to £40 (25 to 51 €)

4 **Ceviche Soho** – *D4* - *17 Frith St. -* ⊖ *Leicester Square or Tottenham Court Road - ℘020 7292 2040 - www. cevicheuk.com - Mon-Thur 12pm-3pm, 5pm-11:30pm, Sat 12pm-11:30pm, Sun 12pm-10.15pm.* Showcasing the best of Peruvian cuisine, the menu offers a delicious choice of ceviche (marinated, spicy fish), and fish and meat from the grill. Enjoy with a pisco infusion cocktail, or classic pisco sour, for the perfect evening in Soho.

44 **Barrafina** – *D4* - *26-27 Dean Street -* ⊖ *Tottenham Court Road ou Leicester Square - ℘020 7813 8016 - www.barrafina.co.uk - Mon-Sat 12pm-3pm, 5pm-11pm, Sun 1pm-3:30pm, 5:30pm-10pm.* A hugely successful, modern take on the Spanish tapas bar. Sit at the counter and watch the skilled chefs prepare plates in front of you. It's advised to arrive early: the space fills quickly and there are no reservations. Two more

sites at Covent Garden, 10 Adelaide Street and 43 Drury Lane.

50 **Hix** – *D4* - *66-70 Brewer St. -* ⊖ *Piccadilly Circus - ℘020 7292 3518 - www.hixsoho.co.uk - Mon-Sat 12pm-11:30pm, Sun 12pm-10:30pm, 24 Dec. 12pm-2pm (lunch time) - Closed 25-26 Dec, 1 Jan.* The more relaxed sister restaurant to British chef, Mark Hix's Mayfair address. The menu is seasonal and champions seafood and shellfish. Pre- and post-theatre food at attractive prices. Cosy cocktail bar below.

COVENT GARDEN

Local map *p. 36*

Under £15 (19 €)

5 **Abeno Too** – *E4* - *17-18 Great Newport St. -* ⊖ *Leicester Square or Covent Garden - ℘020 7379 1160 - www.abeno.co.uk - 12pm-10:30pm (Fri-Sat 11pm, Sun-Mon 10pm).* The speciality of this unpretentious Japanese canteen is the okonomiyaki – a cabbage cake filled with meat, fish or vegetables, cooked directly on a hot plate at your table. Lunch menu at £13.50.

From £35 to £55 (45 to 70 €)

☺ 48 **Rules** – *E4* - *34-35 Maiden Lane -* ⊖ *Covent Garden - ℘020 7836 5314 - www.rules.co.uk - 12pm-12am - Closed 25-26 Dec.* Classic, British cooking, rabbit leg, pork cheeks and game are all on the menu. One of the oldest and most famous restaurants in London, this space is full of history. Reservations advised.

117

🍴

THE STRAND

Local map p. 36

From £30 to £50 (38 to 64 €)

49 Simpson's-in-the-Strand – *E4* -
100 The Strand - ⊖ *Charing Cross -*
📞*020 7836 9112 - www.simpsons
inthestrand.co.uk - Mon-Fri, 7.15am-
10:30am, 12pm-2.45pm, 5:45pm-
10:30pm, Sat 12pm-10:30pm, Sun
12pm-9pm - Knight's Bar Mon-Sat
11am-11pm; Sun, 12pm-9pm.* Sitting
pretty on the Strand since 1828, this
London institution is renowned for its
roasts. Although recently updated,
it remains traditionally British, with
classic food and precise service
delivered under the high ceilings of
the elegant dining room.

THE CITY

Local map p. 50-51

Under £15 (19 €)

6 City Càphê – *G3-4* -
17 Ironmonger Lane - ⊖ *Bank -
www.citycaphe.com - Mon-Fri
11:30am-4:30pm.* A small Vietnamese
establishment that is popular with
City workers, as evidenced by the
queue that forms on the pavement
most lunchtimes. On the menu: banh
mi baguette sandwiches, pho soups,
rolls, and salads served with noodles
or rice. Go after 1.30pm in order to
beat the hordes.

From £15 to £25 (19 to 32 €)

7 Café Below – *G4* - *St Mary-le-
Bow Church, Cheapside -* ⊖ *Mansion
House, Bank or St Paul's -* 📞*020 7329
0789 - www.cafebelow.co.uk -*
*Mon-Tue, 7:30am-2:30pm;
Wed-Fri 7:30am-2:30pm, 5:30pm
-9:30pm.* The historical surroundings
of the thousand year old crypt of
St Mary-le-Bow church (⚓*p. 54*),
houses a restaurant with open
kitchen. Freshly cooked breakfasts
and lunches, using seasonal produce,
are made to eat in or takeaway.

From £25 to £50 (32 to 64 €)

35 Sweetings – *G4* - *39 Queen
Victoria St. -* ⊖ *Mansion House -*
📞*020 7248 3062 - www.sweetings
restaurant.com - Mon-Fri 11:30am-3pm
- closed bank holidays.* Serving
excellent fish and seafood to City
types since 1889. Open for lunch only.
Sit up at the buzzy counter when the
food hall is full.

SOUTHWARK

Local map p. 66-67

Under £15 (19 €)

🌿 8 Borough Market – *G5* -
8 Southwark Street - ⊖ *London
Bridge -* 📞*020 7407 1002 -www.
boroughmarket.org.uk - Wed-Thur
10am-5pm; Fri 10am-6pm; Sat
8am-5pm.* Enjoy a gastronomic tour
around one of the best food markets
in London, taking in the sights and
smells of a huge variety of gourmet
goods as you go. There is something
for every taste and every pocket.
Enjoy your purchases on the move or
find a spot in front of the regularly run
cooking demonstrations at the Demo
Kitchen on the corner of Borough
High St. and Bedale St. If you prefer
your own table, there are many great

© Jon Arnold Images/hemis.fr

119

Borough Market

eateries to choose from in and around the market (see two of the most interesting, below).

From £20 to £25 (26 to 32 €)

9 **Arabica** – *G5* - 3 Rochester Walk, Borough Market - ⊖ London Bridge - ℘020 3011 5151 - www. arabicabarandkitchen.com - Mon-Wed 11am-11pm, Thur-Sat 8:30am-11pm, Sun 11am-4pm. Under the vaults of Borough Market, this large modern Lebanese restaurant is hugely popular at lunchtime. And for good reason, the dishes are fresh and tasty: mezze, grilled meats, all sorts of Turkish breads and pastries from the clay oven and charcoal kebabs. All finished with a mint tea, prepared in the traditional fashion.

😊 **33** **Fish!** – *G5* - Cathedral St., Borough Market - ⊖ London Bridge - ℘020 7407 3803 - www.fishkitchen. com - ♿ - Mon-Fri 11:30am-11pm, Sat 9am-11pm, Sun 10am-10:30pm. The Borough location of this small chain has an open kitchen serving, as the name suggests, all kinds of fresh fish. You can choose how it is cooked.

SOUTH BANK

***Local map** p. 66-67*

Under £15 (19 €)

10 **Southbank Centre Food Market** – *E5* - Belvedere Road - ⊖ Waterloo - ℘020 7960 4200 - www.borough market.org.uk - Fri 12pm-8pm, Sat 11am-8pm, Sun and bank holidays)

12pm-6pm. From Friday to Sunday, food trucks and cooking stalls with cuisines from around the world are set up behind the South Bank Centre. Eat on-site or take-out and enjoy in the Jubilee Gardens along the Thames.

From £45 to £80 (58 to 102 €)

42 Oxo Tower Restaurant & Brasserie – *F4* - *Oxo Tower Wharf, Barge House St. -* ⊖ *Southwark or Blackfriars - ℘020 7803 3888 - www.harveynichols.com/restaurant/the-oxo-tower/ - 12pm-11pm - Closed 25 Dec.* On the top floor of the Oxo Tower (♿p. 65), this restaurant has extraordinary panoramic views. A slick, professional set up – and there is also a summer terrace.

KNIGHTSBRIDGE

Local map *p. 72-73*

From £25 to £45 (32 to 58€)

54 Zuma – *B5* - *5 Raphael St. -* ⊖ *Knightsbridge - ℘020 7584 1010 - www.zumarestaurant.com -* ♿ *- Mon-Fri 12pm-2:30pm, 6pm-9:30pm, Sat-Sun, 12pm-3pm, 6pm-9:30pm, bar 11.15pm - Closed 25 Dec.* This seductive Japanese restaurant is a twist on an izakaya (informal Japanese eatery). Its sleek, contemporary interior and modern menu attracts a stylish crowd. Sit at low cedar tables or up at the counter and snack on sushi, maki, yakitori, tempura and other dishes from the robata grill. The drinks list offers more than 40 sakes.

16 Amaya – *C6* - *Halkin Arcade, 19 Motcomb St. -* ⊖ *Knightsbridge - ℘020 7823 1166 - www.amaya.biz -* ♿ *- Mon-Sat, 12:30pm-3pm, 5:30pm-11:30pm, Sun 12.45pm-3pm, 5:30pm-10:30pm.* This stylish address offers Indian cuisine acclaimed by critics, and rightly so. Michelin-starred, theatre-style cooking rooted in traditional techniques.

CHELSEA AND SOUTH KENSINGTON

Local map *p. 72-73*

Under £15 (19 €)

11 The V&A Café – *B6* - *Victoria and Albert Museum - Cromwell Road -* ⊖ *South Kensington - ℘020 7942 2000 - www.vam.ac.uk -* ♿ *- 10am-5pm (Fri, 9:30pm) - Closed Dec-Jan holidays.* One of many museums in London with a good café offering. The V&A is a must-visit during a stay in London, and the café is located in the oldest and most beautiful part of the building, with its own sunny courtyard. At lunch there are salads, sandwiches, wraps or soups at reasonable prices. Scones and pastries at any time.

12 Jakobs – *A6* - *20 Gloucester Rd -* ⊖ *Gloucester Rd or High Street Kensington - ℘020 7581 9292 - www.jakobs.co.uk - 8pm-11pm.* For those looking for lunch between visits to the museums of South Kensington, this small Armenian establishment offers a well-stocked deli-counter of flavoursome Middle Eastern and Mediterranean salads, mezzes and vegetable dishes. Cheaper to take away.

From £15 to £30 (19 to 38 €)

㉔ Builders Arms – *B7* -
13 Britten St. - ⊖ *Sloane Square -*
✆*020 7349 9040 - www.thebuilders
armskensington.co.uk -* ♿ *- Mon-
Fri 12pm-11pm, Sat 10am-11pm, Sun
12pm-10:30pm.* Eat at this modern
pub seated in comfy armchairs in the
large, library-like dining room.

From £20 to £35 (25 to 45 €)

⑳ Bluebird – *A8* - *350 King's Rd
-* ⊖ *South Kensington -* ✆*020 7559
1000 - www.bluebird-restaurant.
co.uk - Mon-Fri 12pm-2:30pm,
6pm-10-30pm, Sat 12pm-3pm,
6pm-1am, Sun 12pm-3pm, 6pm-11pm.*
Terence Conran's gastrodome
includes a brasserie and design
restaurant serving modern British
cuisine (♿*p. 185*). Great brunch on
weekends.

From £30 to £50 (38 to 64 €)

☺ ⑲ Bibendum Restaurant – *B6* -
Michelin House - 81 Fulham Rd - ⊖
South Kensington - ✆*020 7581 5817 -
www.bibendum.co.uk - Restaurant :
12pm-2:30pm (Sat-Sun 12:30pm-3pm),
6:30pm-10:30pm (Sun 10pm); Oyster
Bar: Mon-Fri 8am-11pm, Sat 9am-11pm,
Sun 12pm-10:30pm.* In this beautiful
Art Nouveau building, where Michelin
once had its offices (♿*p. 76*), comes
exacting, modern French cooking.
Oyster Bar on ground floor.

HYDE PARK

From £20 to £45 (25 to 58 €)

㊳ The Magazine Restaurant – *B5* -
West Carriage Dr. - ⊖ *Hyde Park
Corner or Lancaster Gate -* ✆*020
7298 7552 - www.magazine-
restaurant.co.uk -* 🅿 ♿ *- Tues-Sun
9am-6pm - Closed Mon (and holidays).*
The cafe at the Serpentine Sackler
Gallery, designed by Zaha Hadid,
looks like a great white spaceship
that has landed in the middle of Hyde
Park. Good fusion cuisine is on the
menu, or you may prefer to just enjoy
the surroundings with a cocktail or
over afternoon tea.

NORTH KENSINGTON

***Local map** p. 72-73*

From £20 to £40 (25 to 51 €)

㊴ Kensington Square Kitchen –
A5 - *9 Kensington Sq. -* ⊖ *High Street
Kensington -* ✆*020 7938 2598 - www.
kensingtonsquarekitchen.co.uk -
8am-4pm - Closed Sun, Easter and
23-28 Dec.* A small neighbourhood
restaurant hidden amongst the trees
on pretty Kensington Square. The
menu includes delicately flavoured
soups, colourful salads and dishes
inspired by the cuisines of the world.
Perfect for brunch.

Ffiona's – *Detachable map A5* -
51 Kensington Church St. - ⊖ *High
Street Kensington -* ✆*020 7937
4152 - www.ffionas.com - Tue-Thur,
6pm-11pm, Fri-Sat 10am-3pm,
6pm-11pm, Sun 10am-3pm,
7pm-10pm.* A warm and welcoming
family restaurant with wooden tables
topped with pot plants and candles.
British comfort food using seasonal
ingredients, with excellent fish and
chips and a tasty lamb with mint.

🍴

NOTTING HILL

Local map p. 83

On Fridays and Saturdays, when the flea market is on, you will find plenty of international food stalls along Portobello Road. Also walk up the street to Golborne Road, a pleasant street lined with cafés and Moroccan food stalls.

From £20 to £40 (25 to 51 €)

40 E&O – *14 Blenheim Crescent – ⊖ Ladbroke Grove - ☎020 7229 5454 - www.rickerrestaurants. com - Mon-Fri, 12pm-3pm, 6pm-11pm, Sat 11am-11pm, Sun 11am-10:30pm.* Contemporary design and lounge music in this bar-restaurant which welcomes a trendy clientele. Asian fusion cuisine.

61 202 – *202 Westbourne Grove - ⊖ Notting Hill Gate - ☎020 7727 2722 - www.202london.com - Mon-Wed, 8:30am-6pm; Thur-Sat 8:30am-10pm; Sun, 10am-5pm - Closed 25-26 Dec.* In the Nicole Fahri store you'll find clothing and homewares in the basement and a lively café-restaurant on the ground floor. International cuisine with good breakfast options.

MARYLEBONE

Local map p. 87

Under £15 (19 €)

55 The Golden Hind – *C3* - *73 Marylebone Lane - ⊖ Bond Street - ☎020 7486 3644 - Mon-Fri, 12pm-3pm, 6pm-10pm, Sat 6pm-10pm.* Serving fish and chips since 1914. Squid, cod, haddock, plaice and other seafood all available. A good lunchtime destination.

From £30 to £50 (38 to 64 €)

60 Chiltern Firehouse – *C3* - *1 Chiltern St. - ⊖ Bond Street or Baker Street - ☎020 7073 7676 - www. chilternfirehouse.com - breakfast (Mon-Fri 7am-10:30am, Sat-Sun 9am-10:30am), brunch (Sat-Sun 11am-3pm), breakfast (Mon-Wed, 12pm-2:30pm, Thur-Fri 12pm-3pm), dinner (Mon-Wed, 5:30pm-10:30pm, Thur-Sun 6pm-10:30pm).* A magnificent former Victorian fire station converted into a luxury hotel and brasserie by the American hotelier André Balazs. Popular with the rich and famous and foodies alike, the food is prepared in a huge open kitchen. This is contemporary British gastronomy; minimalist, delicious and refined. Booking is recommended.

BLOOMSBURY

From £20 to £45 (25 to 58 €)

45 Lima Fitzrovia – *D3* - *31 Rathbone Pl. - ⊖ Tottenham Court Road - ☎020 3002 2640 - www.limafitzrovia.com - Mon-Sat 12pm-2:30pm, 5:30pm-10pm, Sun 12pm-3pm - Closed bank holidays.* The chef Virgilio Martinez concocts new Peruvian cuisine of the highest quality. Dishes are light, subtly designed and a delicate balance of taste, texture and colour. The lunch menu is good value. An intimate space, reservations recommended.

52 **Dabbous** – *D3* - *39 Whitfield St. - Goodge Street - ☎020 7323 1544 - www.dabbous.co.uk - Mon-Sat 12pm-2pm, 6pm-9:30pm - Closed Sun, Easter and 25 Dec.* In this industrial setting, delicious plates are dished up, such as fennel and lemon salad, rose petal chips, monkfish and Jerusalem artichoke, beef tartare mayonnaise and tarragon. The atmospheric cocktail bar in the basement also offers snacks. Booking necessary.

KING'S CROSS

From £15 to £30 (19 to 38 €)

17 **Dishoom King's Cross** – *E1* - *5 Stable St. - King's Cross St Pancras - ☎020 7420 9321 - www.dishoom.com - ♿ - Mon-Wed, 8am-11pm; Thur-Fri, 8am-12am; Sat 9am-12am, Sun 9pm-11pm.* Before heading to the Eurostar, or taking a stroll around the newly regenerated King's Cross quarter (♿ p.92), dine at this superb Indian restaurant. Inspired by the old Irani cafés of Bombay, the food is fresh and perfectly spiced, with cocktails and fruit lassis to drink. A perfect weekday lunch venue. Other locations in Covent Garden, 12 Upper St. Martin's Lane, and Shoreditch, 7 Boundary St.

From £35 to £55 (45 to 70 €)

21 **German Gymnasium** – *E1* - *1 King's Boulevard - King's Cross St Pancras - ☎020 7287 8000 - www.germangymnasium.com - ♿ - Restaurant: 12pm-3pm, 6pm-11pm; Grand Café: Mon-Fri 8am-10pm; Sat-Sun, 10am-10pm.* One of the standout refurbishment projects in King's

© Thomas Alexander Photography/D&D London

German Gymnasium

Cross, this former gymnasium, built in 1865 for the training of the German gymnastics team, now houses an impressive, chic restaurant. German chef Bjoern Wassmuth is at the helm. Unlimited coffee with breakfast.

CAMDEN TOWN

***Local map** p. 94*

At the weekend, world food stalls pop up along **Camden Lock** and **Stables Antique Market.** Treat yourself to authentic curry, sushi, noodles, chilli con carne or *maafe* (African peanut stew) for a fraction of the price you would find in a restaurant.

🍴

From £15 to £20 (19 to 25 €)

22 **Poppie's** – *730 Hawley Crescent - ⊖ Camden Town - ✆020 7267 0440 - www.poppiesfishandchips.co.uk - 11am-12am (Sun 11pm).* Fresh fish, generous chip portions, all within walking distance from lively Camden. What more could you ask for?

HAMPSTEAD

Most of the pubs mentioned in our *Beverages* section (♿p.131) are also good for food.

Under £15 (19 €)

Ginger & White – *Detachable map - 4a-5a Perrins Court - ⊖ Hampstead - ✆020 7431 9098 - www.gingerand white.com - Mon-Fri 7:30am-5:30pm, Sat-Sun, 8:30am-5:30pm.* Situated in one of Hampstead's pretty antiques-laden alleys. Popular with locals for its good coffee and fresh and original all-day breakfasts. Perfect before or after a walk on the heath.

From £25 to £30 (32 to 38 €)

The Wells – *Detachable map - 30 Well Walk - ⊖ Hampstead - ✆020 7794 3785 - www.thewellshampstead. co.uk. 12pm-11pm (10:30pm).* One of the oldest pubs in Hampstead, and arguably the most popular. The bar downstairs attracts a young crowd, while the first floor dining rooms offer a gastropub experience. Charming and friendly.

EAST END

Local map p. 98-99

Under £15 (19 €)

23 **Beigel Shop** – *H2 - 155 Brick Lane - ⊖ Shoreditch High Street (Overground) or Liverpool Street - ✆020 7729 0826 - 24 hours, 7 days a week.* A Brick Lane institution, known as '*the yellow one*' by locals. People come back to buy the famous, freshly-made bagels. Now also serving rainbow bagels!

13 **Old Spitalfields Market** – *H3 - Angle Commercial St./Brushfield St. - ⊖ Liverpool Street - ✆020 7377 1496 - www.spitalfields.co.uk - ♿ - stands and food trucks : 10am-19pm; restaurants: Mon-Fri 8am-11pm, Sat-Sun 9am-11pm.* The Spitalfields Market (♿p. 100) has daily food trucks and food stalls that are great for low-cost meal options. It also hosts various food events that attract visiting gourmets. There are several restaurants in the hall, including Canteen, which specialises in English cuisine.

18 **Bengal Village** – *H3 - 75 Brick Lane - ⊖ Shoreditch High Street (Overground) or Liverpool Street - ✆020 7366 4868 - www.bengal village.com - ♿ - 12pm-11:30pm.* A renowned curry house on Brick Lane, regarded by many as one of the best in the area. It has a contemporary look and traditional menu boasting many regional specialties from Bangladesh, including plenty of great vegetarian dishes.

From £20 to £35 (€ 25 to 45)

56 **The Princess of Shoreditch** – *H2* - *76-78 Paul St. - ⊖ Old Street - ℰ020 7729 9270 - www.theprincessof shoreditch.com - Mon-Fri 12pm-3pm, 6:30pm-10pm, Sat 12pm-4pm, 6:30pm-10pm, Sun 12pm-9pm.* A good example of a gastropub – seasonal roasts, pies and fish dishes are made with care. Accompanied by good blonde and light beers.

From £25 to £40 (€ 32 to 51)

27 **Brawn** – *H2* - *49 Columbia Rd - ⊖ Hoxton (Overground) - ℰ020 7729 5692 - www.brawn.co - Mon 6pm-11pm, Tue-Sat 12pm-3pm, 6pm-11pm, Sun 12pm-4pm.* In the open kitchen of this good-looking centre of gastronomy an exacting approach is taken to sourcing the best seasonal ingredients. The food is unpretentious, fresh and delicious. Take advantage of the three-course Sunday lunch menu (£28) as part of a trip to Columbia Road Flower Market (♿p. 139). Reservations are highly recommended.

DOCKLANDS

***Local map** p. 104-105*

From £20 to £35 (25 to 45 €)

28 **The Gun** – *27 Coldharbour - ⊖ Canary Wharf - ℰ020 7515 5222 - www.thegundocklands.com - &. - Mon-Fri 12pm-3pm, 6pm-10:30pm, Sat-Sun 12pm-4pm, 6pm-10:30pm (Sun 9:30pm) - Closed 25 Dec.* On the banks of the Thames, in the shadow of modern waterside developments, lies this historic 18th Century pub.

Refined cuisine and decor with Fuller's beer on tap.

GREENWICH

***Local map** p. 104-105*

Under £15 (19 €)

29 **Greenwich Market** - *⊖ Cutty Sark - ℰ020 8305 9612 - www. greenwichmarketlondon.com - Tues-Sun 10am-5:30pm.* To eat well without spending a fortune, take advantage of the international food stalls found amongst the craft and design stands at Greenwich market. Pick up a bite and take it to enjoy by the Thames, under the masts of the Cutty Sark.

30 **Goddards at Greenwich** - *22 King William Walk - ⊖ Cutty Sark - ℰ020 8305 9612 - www. goddardsatgreenwich.co.uk - 10am-7pm (Fri-Sat 8pm, Sun 7:30pm).* Established in 1890, this traditional pie and mash shop has been serving the British speciality for hundreds of years. Minced beef pie with mash and liquor (a salty parsley sauce), along with other meat and veg options, plus gluten free. Considered one of the best pie and mash joints in London.

70 **Royal Teas Café** - *76 Royal Hill - ⊖ Greenwich - ℰ020 8691 7240 - www.royalteascafe. co.uk - 9:30am-5:30pm (Sun 10:30am-5:30pm).* Nestled in a quiet street, this charming café is a warm and welcoming place to indulge in delicious homemade food accompanied by good coffee, tea or hot chocolate. Light vegetarian dishes also available for lunch (soups, salads, tarts etc).

Where to drink

♿ *Locate the addresses on our plans with numbered pads (ex. ①). The coordinates in red (ex. C2) refer to the detachable plan.*

HAVE A CUP OF TEA

Nowhere is the British tradition of afternoon tea more celebrated than London. Make the most of your stay and enjoy the ritual for yourself (♿ p. 184).

ST JAMES'S

Local map p. 25

126

① **The Ritz London** – *D5* - 150 Piccadilly - ⊖ Green Park - ☎020 7493 8181 - www.theritzlondon.com - Tea service: 11:30am, 1:30pm, 3:30pm, 5:30pm and 7:30pm. The world-renowned hotel, frequented by politicians, film stars and royalty, is well-known for its special afternoon tea served in the stunning Palm Court. You have to book about six weeks in advance, but the experience is unforgettable (£52). Note: no jeans or sports shoes allowed and a jacket and tie is required for men.

② **Fortnum & Mason's Restaurants** – *D4* - 181 Piccadilly - ⊖ Piccadilly Circus - ☎020 7205 45 45 - www.fortnumandmason.co.uk - ♿ - Afternoon tea: 3pm-5pm - Closed Sun, Easter and 25 Dec. The famous food emporium has several restaurants where you can indulge in afternoon tea. The most popular are the Fountain (level one) and the very

smart and very pricy Diamond Jubilee (level four) - from £40, reservation recommended. Chic attire required.

MAYFAIR

Local map p. 28-29

④ **Claridge's** – *C4* - Brook St. - ⊖ Bond Street - ☎020 7107 8886 - www.claridges.co.uk - Tea service: 2.45pm-5:30pm; reservations only - Closed 25 Dec. This five-star address has an equally special afternoon tea offering with all the trimmings. Set in stunning Art Deco surroundings. Chic attire required.

COVENT GARDEN

Local map p. 36

⑱ **Primrose Bakery** – *E4* - 42 Tavistock St. - ⊖ Covent Garden or Temple - ☎020 7836 3638 - www.primrose-bakery.co.uk - Mon-Sat 10am-7:30pm, Sun 12pm-5pm. Tea time offers the perfect opportunity to try the delicious cupcakes from this famous bakery. Topped with multicoloured icing, flavours include vanilla, chocolate, caramel, coffee, carrot cake or red velvet.

THE STRAND

Local map p. 36

③ **The Savoy** – *E4* - The Strand - ⊖ Charing Cross or Covent Garden - ☎ 020 7836 4343 - www.fairmont.com/savoy-london/- 🅿 -

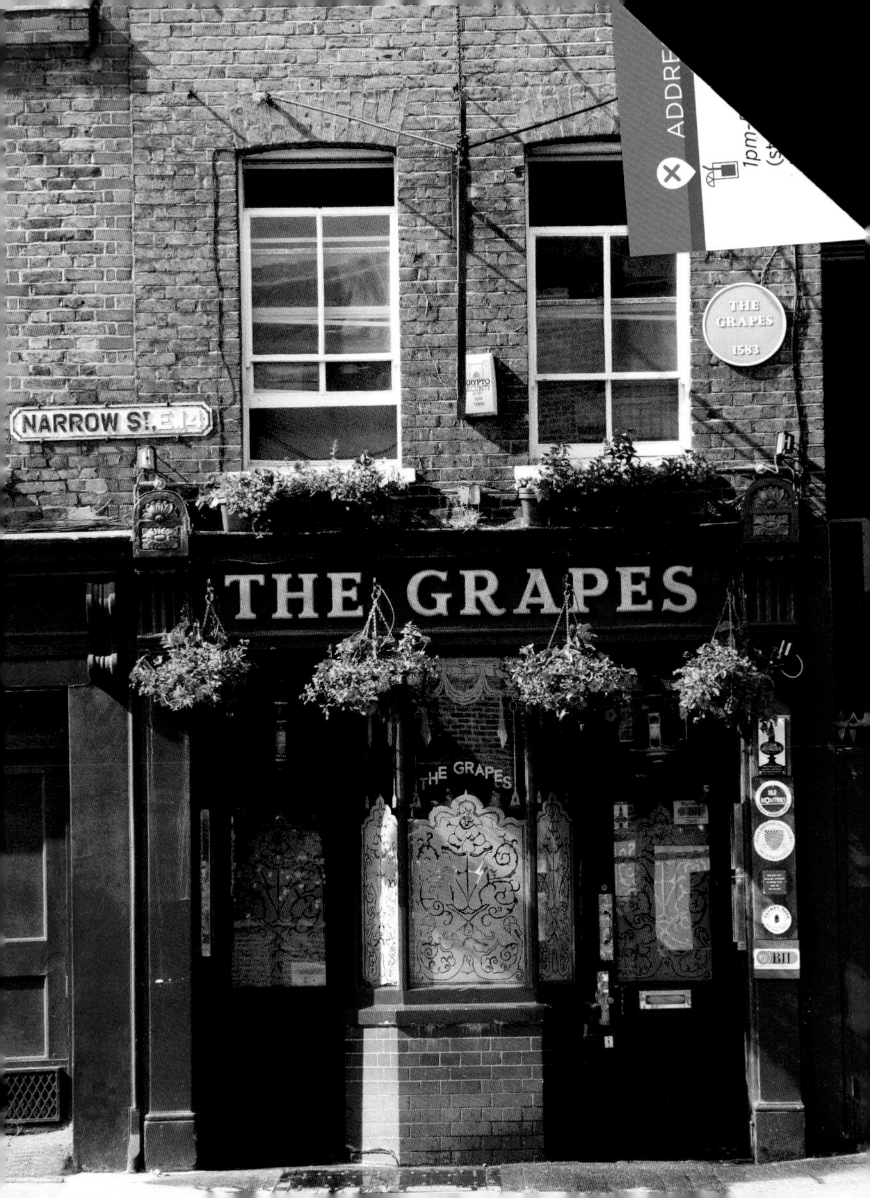
NARROW St. E.14
THE GRAPES
1583
THE GRAPES
THE GRAPES

5:45pm. A unique experience (starting from £50) in an exceptional hotel. Booking essential up to six weeks in advance for weekends. Compulsory dress code.

KNIGHTSBRIDGE AND SOUTH KENSINGTON

Local map p. 72-73

5 **Harrods - The Tea Room** – *B5* - 135 Brompton Rd - ⊖ Knightsbridge - ☏020 7730 1234 - www.harrods.com - **P** £20/2hrs - ♿ - Mon-Sat, 10am-9pm; Sun 11:30am-6pm; Sun and Easter, 12pm-6pm; No reservations. Between purchases, go to the second floor of the store for a delicious afternoon tea. Traditional (£29) or champagne (♿ *p. 70*).

St Stephen's Tavern, Westminster

© Ch. Heeb/hemis.fr

19 **The Orangery** – *A5* - Kensington Palace, Kensington Gardens - ⊖ Queensway, Notting Hill Gate or High Street Kensington - ☏020 3166 6113 - www.orangerykensingtonpalace. co.uk - ♿ - 12pm-6pm - closures according to events, check website -No reservations. Have afternoon tea (£27.50) in the light and airy surroundings of the 18th Century orangery at Kensington Palace (♿ *p.80*). A perfect place to rest in the heart of the park.

DRINK A BEER

The British pub is the descendant of medieval inns and taverns. Many of the public houses still around today are several centuries old and retain many of their original decorative features. They can play an important role in British social lives, and act as a meeting place for friends, work colleagues and sports fans. Draught beer is served by the pint or half pint, and is often also available in bottles.

WESTMINSTER

Local map p. 17

7 **St Stephen's Tavern** – *E5* - 10 Bridge St. - ⊖ Westminster - ☏020 7925 2286 - www.ststephens tavern.co.uk - 10am-11:30pm, Sun 10am-10:30pm. Facing Big Ben Tower, this lovely Victorian pub, with its cosy atmosphere, is a pleasant stop on a tour around the Westminster area.

ST JAMES'S

Local map p. 25

8 **Golden Lion** – *D5* - *25 King St. -* ⊖ *Green Park* - *☎020 7925 0007 - www.goldenlion-stjames.co.uk - Mon-Fri 11am-11pm, Sat 12pm-6pm - Closed Sun* Even if the neighbouring St James theatre has long since disappeared, this pub dating back to 1762 remains an institution.

SOHO

Local map p. 28-29

9 **Argyll Arms** – *D3* - *18 Argyll St. -* ⊖ *Oxford Circus* - *☎020 7734 6117 - www.nicholsonspubs.co.uk - 10am-11:30pm.* This historic pub (est. 1716) has retained its superb 18th Century decor, with huge mirrors, carved woodwork and ornate ceilings, and a mahogany wood bar. Its location in the lively Oxford Circus area also explains its popularity.

COVENT GARDEN

Local map p. 36

10 **Lamb & Flag** – *E4* - *33 Rose St. -* ⊖ *Covent Garden* - *☎020 7497 9504 - www.lambandflag-covent garden.co.uk - Mon-Sat 11am-11pm, Sun 12pm-10:30pm.* Nestled in a narrow alley, the oldest tavern in the area (est. 1623) continues to attract a crowd of regulars and tourists thanks to a cosy and friendly atmosphere and a good selection of beers.

11 **The Globe** – *E4* - *37 Bow St. -* ⊖ *Covent Garden* - *☎020 7379 0154 www.theglobebowstreet.co.uk -*

&. *- Mon-Thur 11am-11:30pm, Fri-Sat 11am-12pm, Sun 11am-10:30pm - Closed 25 Dec.* Established in 1682, The Globe is one of Bow Street's eight historic pubs. There is no lack of character, with lots of original woodwork, and the atmosphere is buzzy in the evening, when the place fills with an eclectic clientele. Roof terrace.

HOLBORN

Local map p. 43

21 **Princess Louise** – *E3* - *208 High Holborn -* ⊖ *Holborn* - *☎020 7405 8816 - www.princesslouisepub.co.uk - &. - Mon-Fri 11am-11pm, Sat 12pm-11pm, Sun 12pm-10:30pm.* This late 19th Century pub, named after Queen Victoria's fourth daughter, is worth a visit for its magnificent Victorian design features.

CLERKENWELL

Local map p. 43

27 **Craft Beer Co** – *F3* - *82 Leather Lane -* ⊖ *Chancery Lane* - *☎020 7834 9988 - www.thecraftbeerco.com - 11am-11pm - Closed 25 Dec.* With the best keg beers from around the world, and over 15 cask ales sourced from microbreweries across the UK, as well as more than 200 bottled beers, this a beer-lover's paradise.

129

THE CITY

***Local map* p. 50-51**

26 The Blackfriar – *F4* - *174 Queen Victoria St. - ⊖ Blackfriars - ☎020 7236 5474 - www.nicholsonspubs. co.uk - Mon-Sat 10am-11pm, Sun 12pm-10:30pm - Closed 24-25 Dec.* Outside Blackfriars tube, in a striking triangular building, this historic pub sits on the site of a former Dominican monastery. The Art Nouveau, Grade II listed building has pretty engravings outside and a good choice of real ales behind the bar inside.

SOUTHWARK

***Local map* p. 66-67**

130 **12 The Anchor Bankside** – *G5* - *34 Park St. - ⊖ London Bridge - ☎020 7407 1577 - www.taylor-walker. co.uk - ♿ - Mon-Sat 11pm-11:30pm; Sun, 12pm-10:30pm.* Rebuilt in 1676 after the Great Fire of London, this historic pub at the foot of Southwark Bridge has a labyrinth of cosy, dark rooms. Pleasant terrace overlooking the Thames.

13 The George Inn – *G5* - *75-77 Borough High St. - ⊖ London Bridge - ☎020 7407 2056 - www.nationaltrust. org.uk/george-inn - Mon-Thur, 11am-11pm; Fri-Sat, 11am-12am; Sun and Bank holidays 12pm-10:30pm.* This pub nestled in a narrow alley off Borough High Street is worth a visit for its unique architecture and aged interior, with many, winding, connecting bar rooms.

KNIGHTSBRIDGE

***Local map* p. 72-73**

14 The Grenadier – *C5* - *18 Wilton Row - ⊖ Knightsbridge or Hyde Park Corner - ☎020 7235 3074 - www. taylor-walker.co.uk - Mon-Sat 12pm-11pm, Sun 12pm-10:30pm.* This historic British pub was frequented by the Duke of Wellington and his grenadiers. Traditional pub food with a good selection of dishes.

CHELSEA

***Local map* p. 72-73**

15 The Pig's Ear – *B8* - *35 Old Church St. - ⊖ Sloane Square - ☎020 7352 2908 - www.thepigsear.info - 12pm-11pm, Sun 12pm-10:30pm.* Located on a quiet street, set off the King's Road, this pub is a bright and pleasant place for a drink in the early evening. Restaurant upstairs.

NOTTING HILL

***Local map* p. 83**

16 The Cow – *89 Westbourne Park Rd - ⊖ Royal Oak - ☎020 7221 0021 - www.thecowlondon.co.uk - 12pm-11pm; Sun 12pm-10:30pm.* One of the nicest pubs in Notting Hill, as any of its clientele of trendy regulars will happily confirm. Beautiful terrace with wooden benches. At the end of the day, you can enjoy a few Guinness oysters or a delicious Irish stew.

CAMDEN TOWN

Local map p. 93

17 **Lock 17** – *11 East Yard, Camden Lock -* 🚇 *Camden Town -* 📞 *020 7428 5929 - www.lock17.com - Mon-Wed 11am-12am, Thur-Sat 11am-2.30am, Sun 11am-11pm - Closed 25 Dec.* In the heart of Camden Lock Market, this funky bar has a pleasant mezzanine and a terrace overlooking the canal.

HAMPSTEAD

The Spaniard's Inn – *Detachable plan* – *Spaniards Rd -* 🚇 *Hampstead or East Finchley and 15min from the market -* 📞 *020 8731 8406 - www.thespaniardshampstead.co.uk -* 🅿 *- 12pm-11pm; Sun 12pm-10:30pm.* This tavern from 1585 sits on the edge of Hampstead Heath, and has a bright atmosphere despite its dark and brooding interior. Terrace with barbecues in summer and entertainment on Saturday evenings.

The Old Bull & Bush – *Detachable plan* – *North End Rd -* 🚇 *Golders Green -* 📞 *020 8905 5456 - www.thebullandbush.co.uk -* 🅿 ♿ *- 11am-11pm, Sun 12pm-10:30pm.* This 1920s building is decorated with paintings of musical hall singer Florrie Forde, who named one of her songs after the establishment. The rest of the venue is modern with smart pub food served from the kitchen.

The Flask – *Detachable plan* – *14 Flask Walk -* 🚇 *Hampstead -* 📞 *020 7435 4580 - www.theflaskhampstead.co.uk - Mon-Thur 11am-11pm, Fri-Sat 11am-12am, Sun 12pm-10:30pm.* In winter, an open fire warms this country-style pub, which counted Karl Marx as one of its regulars.

EAST END

Local map p. 98-99

24 **The Ten Bells** – *H3* – *84 Commercial St. -* 🚇 *Liverpool Street -* 📞 *020 7247 7532 - www.tenbells.com - 12pm-12am (Thur-Sat 1am).* This historic Spitalfields pub, located in front of the market, is known to have been the lair of Jack the Ripper. A superb decor of ceramics and restored woodwork attracts City types and tourists alike.

DOCKLANDS

Local map p. 104-105

20 **Prospect of Whitby** – *57 Wapping Wall -* 🚇 *Wapping -* 📞 *020 7481 1095 - 12pm-11pm, Fri-Sat 12pm-12am, Sun 12pm-10:30pm.* This vast, delightfully old-fashioned pub is one of the most touristy on the banks of the Thames. Built in 1553, it is said to have been visited by Samuel Pepys. The terrace offers a beautiful view of the river.

22 **The Grapes** – *Limehouse - 76 Narrow St. -* 🚇 *Westferry (DLR) -* 📞 *020 7987 4396 - www.thegrapes.co.uk - 12pm-11pm, Sun 12pm-10:30pm - Closed 24-25 Dec.* This charming historic public house, formerly frequented by Dickens, has two tiny terraces overlooking the Thames. Bar food downstairs and a fine dining room upstairs.

🛍 *Shopping*

Whatever your style or budget, you'll find something of interest in the many and varied shopping districts of London – whether that's the well-known high street retailers of Oxford Street or high end stores of Knightsbridge, the luxury leather goods, art dealers and fashion designers of Bond Street, vintagewares of the East End, Notting Hill and Camden, or the quirky shops of Seven Dials, northeast of Covent Garden, not to mention the museum shops.

♿ *Locate the addresses on our plans with numbered pads (ex. ①). The coordinates in red (ex. C2) refer to the detachable plan.*

ST JAMES'S

***Local map** p. 24*

Tailors

㉔ Hilditch & Key – *D4* - *73 Jermyn St. - ⊖ Green Park - ✆020 7930 5336 - www.hilditchandkey.co.uk - Mon-Sat 9:30am-6pm (Sat 10am).* Located on the legendary Jermyn Street, lies one of the oldest shirtmakers in the city. Buy ready-to-wear or customised. Womenswear also available.

Hats

⑧ Lock & Co. Hatters – *D5* - *6 St James's St. - ⊖ Green Park - ✆020 7930 8874 - www.lockhatters. co.uk - Mon-Fri 9am-5:30pm, Sat 9:30am-5pm.* Opened in 1759, this historic St James's Street hatter has capped the world's great names, from Admiral Lord Nelson and Jacqueline Kennedy to Charlie Chaplin, Winston Churchill and Oscar Wilde, who left a debt of £3.30! Furnish yourself with a quality bowler, top hat, woollen cap or trilby.

Department Stores

④ Fortnum & Mason – *D4* - *181 Piccadilly - ⊖ Green Park or Piccadilly Circus - ✆0845 300 1707 - www.fortnumandmason.com - 10am-8pm, Sun 11:30am-6pm.* One of the oldest and grandest food stores (♿p. 30). Incredible choice of teas, biscuits, confectionery, spirits, etc.They even produce their own honey.

Fashion, Decoration

㊲ Cath Kidston – *D4* - *French Railways House, 178-180 Piccadilly - ⊖ Piccadilly Circus - ✆020 7499 9895 - www.cathkidston.com - Mon-Sat, 10am-8pm; Sun 12pm-6pm - Closed Dec and Easter.* Over three floors, the colourful floral universe of this designer includes decorative objects, clothes, fabrics, accessories, beauty products and items for the home.

Tins of tea, Fortnum & Mason

MAYFAIR AND PICCADILLY

Local map **p. 28-29**

Womens Fashion

5 **Vivienne Westwood** – *C4* -
6 Davies St. - ⊖ Bond Street - ✆020
7629 3757 - www.viviennewestwood.
co.uk - Mon-Sat 10am-6pm, Thur
10am-7pm. The temple of Queen Viv,
punk icon and fashion legend.

6 **Stella McCartney** – *D4* -
30 Bruton St. - ⊖ Green Park - ✆020
7518 3100 - www.stellamccartney.com
- Mon-Sat 10am-7pm - Closed Easter
and 25 Dec. The creations of the
talented Stella are not within reach of
all budgets, but the shop is worth a
visit just for the experience.

Shoes

41 **Charlotte Olympia** – *D4* -
56 Maddox St.- ⊖ Bond Street -
✆020 7499 0145 - www.charlotte
olympia.com - Mon-Sat 10am-6pm
(Thur 7pm). The big name in luxury
shoe design offers distinctively
extravagant footwear with old school
glamour and a touch of humour.

SOHO

Local map **p. 28-29**

Department Stores

7 **Liberty** – *D4* - Great Malborough
St. - ⊖ Oxford Circus - ✆020 7734
1234 - www.liberty.co.uk - Mon-Sat
10am-8pm, Sun 12pm-6pm. Behind a

splendid Tudor facade stands one of London's most famous shops (♿ *p. 32*). The third floor features the store's famous floral print fabrics. Much of the merchandise is very expensive, but the visual treat of the interior justifies a visit.

Shoes

10 Irregular Choice – *D4* - *35 Carnaby St. -* ⊖ *Piccadilly Circus or Oxford Circus -* ✆*020 7494 4811 - www. irregularchoice.com -* ♿ *- Mon-Sat 10am-8pm, Sun 11am-7pm.* The flagship store of this quirky brand is a Carnaby Street institution. The shop is colourful, glamorous and original, and so are the shoes.

28 Hunter – *D4* - *83-85 Regent St. -* ⊖ *Piccadilly Circus -* ✆*020 7287 2999 - www.hunterboots.com - Mon-Sat 10am-8pm, Sun 1pm-6pm.* The home of the well-known, high-end wellies. Choose from many colours, patterns and styles.

134

Magazines, Records

11 Vintage Magazine Shop – *D4* - *39-43 Brewer St. -* ⊖ *Piccadilly Circus -* ✆*020 7439 8525 - www.vinmag.com - Mon-Thur, 10am-8pm; Fri-Sat 10am-10pm, Sun 12pm-6pm.* Selling vintage comics, science fiction, fashion and movie magazines since 1975. You'll also find old cinema posters and newer movie-based paraphenalia and figurines.

12 Berwick Street – *D4* - *Berwick St. -* ⊖ *Piccadilly Circus.* This buzzy street is known for its market and its many specialist (new or used) record stores. At no.30 is the famous Reckless Records, which stocks second hand vinyl of all genres.

At no.75, Sister Ray, which specialises in indie rock.

Toys

38 Hamleys – *D4* - *188-196 Regent St. -* ⊖ *Piccadilly or Oxford Circus -* ✆*0371 704 1977 - www.hamleys.com - Mon-Fri, 10am-9pm; Sat, 9:30am-9pm; Sun, 12pm-6pm - Closed Sun, Easter holidays.* Return to your childhood and take a tour of this fairytale store. Set over seven floors, it is one of the largest toy shops in the world and offers a shopping experience full of magic and fun.

Fashion, Deco

39 Anthropologie – *D4* - *158 Regent St. -* ⊖ *Piccadilly Circus -* ✆*020 7529 9800 - www.anthropologie.eu -* ♿ *- Mon-Sat 10am-7pm (Thur to 8pm), Sun 12pm-6pm - Closed Easter and 25 Dec.* The first European shop from the American brand offers a range of women's clothing and accessories, and homewares from interesting independent makers. There are also quirky pieces of interest from lesser-known London designers.

Confectionery

44 M & M's World – *D4* - *Swiss Court, 1 Leicester Square -* ⊖ *Leicester Square or Piccadilly Circus -* ✆*020 7025 7171 - www.mmsworld.com -* ♿ *- Mon-Sat, 10am-12am; Sun 12pm-6:30pm - Closed Easter and 25 Dec.* The flagship store for the chocolate *that melts in the mouth not in the hand.* Four floors overlook touristy Leicester Square, and attracts the crowds. Clothes, accessories, gadgets and, of course, vast quantities of M&M's which are kept in huge multicoloured tubes.

COVENT GARDEN

Local map **p. 36**

Cheeses

14 **Neal's Yard Dairy** – *E4* - *17 Shorts Gardens -* ⊖ *Covent Garden -* ☎*020 7240 5700 - www.nealsyarddairy. co.uk -* ♿ *- Mon-Sat 10am-7pm - Closed Sun, 25 Dec, 1 Jan.* Discover more than 50 varieties of gourmet cheese, including the best examples of British classics; cheddar and stilton.

Jewellery, Accessories

40 **Tatty Devine** – *E4* - *44 Monmouth St. -* ⊖ *Covent Garden -* ☎*020 7836 2685 - www.tattydevine. com - Mon-Sat, 10:30am-7pm; Sun 11:30am-5pm.* Established by two British creatives, this independent boutique is famous for its eccentric, perspex jewellery and name necklaces. It also offers personalised designs, decorated with charms, that are made while you wait.

Cosmetics

15 **Neal's Yard Remedies** – *E3* - *15 Neal's Yard -* ⊖ *Covent Garden -* ☎*020 7379 7222 - www. nealsyardremedies.com -* ♿ *- Mon-Sat 10am-8pm; Sun, 11am-6pm - Closed Easter and 25 Dec.* The founding store of the pioneering organic cosmetics brand, which now has outlets across the UK. Explore the range and enjoy a little pampering in the therapy room while you shop.

Books

13 **Magma** – *E3* - *29 Shorts Gardens -* ⊖ *Covent Garden -* ☎ *020 7240 8498 - www.magma-shop.com - Mon-Sat, 11am-7pm; Sun, 12pm-6pm - Closed 1 Jan, 25-26 Dec.*

Large selection of books on design, typography, fashion, illustration and modern art.

TEMPLE

Local map **p. 43**

Tea

16 **Twinings** – *F4* - *216 The Strand -* ⊖ *Temple or Charing Cross -* ☎*020 7353 3511 - www.twinings.co.uk -* ♿ *- Mon-Fri, 9:30am-7pm; Sat, 10am-5pm, Sun 10:30am-4:30pm - Closed 25-26 Dec.* Founded 300 years ago, the flagship store of the famous tea brand still offers blends of all flavours and infusions. As well as the historical shelves there is also a modern tea bar for tastings and masterclasses.

SOUTHWARK

Local map **p. 66-67**

Market

17 **Borough Market** – *G5* - *8 Southwark St.- Borough High St. -* ⊖ *London Bridge -* ☎*020 7407 1002 - www.boroughmarket.org.uk - Wed-Thur, 10am-5pm; Fri, 10am-6pm, Sat, 8am-5pm.* The oldest food market in the capital remains very popular, offering fine foods and rustic specialities from around England, with a focus on organic and quality ingredients. Head there for a taste of the atmosphere and the gourmet treats on offer (♿ *p. 61 and 119)*.

SOUTH BANK

Local map *p. 66-67*

Fashion, Deco

45 **Oxo Tower Wharf** – *F4* - *Barge House St.-* ⊖ *Southwark or Blackfriars -* ℘*020 7021 1686 - www. oxotower.co.uk - Tue-Sun, 11am-6pm.* Ceramics, jewellery, textiles, lighting, gadgets. Designers and craftsmen trade across three floors of the former Oxo building (♿ *p. 65).*

BELGRAVIA AND KNIGHTSBRIDGE

Local map *p. 72-73*

Department Stores

1 **Harvey Nichols** – *C5* - *109-125 Knightsbridge -* ⊖ *Knightsbridge -* ℘*020 7235 5000 - www.harvey nichols.com - 10am-9pm, Sun 11:30am-6pm.* You will find the biggest fashion brands, beauty products and home accessories in this great department store (♿*p. 70).* There is also a high-end food shop which specialises in unusual products, from the UK and elsewhere.

2 **Harrods** – *B5* - *87-135 Brompton Rd -* ⊖ *Knightsbridge -* ℘*020 7730 1234 - www.harrods.com - Mon-Sat 10am-9pm, Sun 11am-6pm - Closed Easter and 25 Dec.* Harrods prides itself on being able to *provide all things for all people, everywhere.* A destination for its unique decor, and landmark status. Its famous food hall is also joined by a hairdressing salon, a beauty institute, travel agency and a shipping service, to name but a few extras (♿ *p. 70).*

CHELSEA AND SOUTH KENSINGTON

Local map *p. 72-73*

Deco

3 **The Conran Shop** – *B6* - *Michelin House - 81 Fulham Rd -* ⊖ *South Kensington -* ℘*020 7589 7401 - www. conranshop.co.uk - Mon-Tue and Fri 10am-6pm, Wed-Thur 10am-7pm, Sat 10am-6:30pm, Sun 12pm-6pm.* The London furniture and decor shop of the famous designer Terence Conran (creator of Habitat).

NOTTING HILL

Local map *p. 83*

Fashion

18 **Paul Smith** – *122 Kensington Park Rd -* ⊖ *Notting Hill Gate -* ℘*020 7727 3553 - www.paulsmith.co.uk - 10am-6pm (Sat to 6:30pm), Sun 12pm-5pm - Closed 25-26 Dec, 1 Jan.* A showroom and boutique, Westbourne House is the elegant address of the famous fashion designer Paul Smith, who lives within walking distance of the address. Set in a private mansion house, visit to see the London creative's collections or buy some pieces for yourself. Books, shoes and accessories also available.

Flea Markets

19 **Portobello Road** – *Portobello Rd -* ⊖ *Notting Hill Gate -* ℘*020 7727 7684 - www.portobelloroad.co.uk - Mon-Wed, 9am-6pm; Thur, 9am-1pm, Fri-Sat, 9am-7pm.* From Notting Hill Gate to the north of Portobello Road

Harrods

there are antique shops, vintage emporiums, jewellery and craft stores and a food market. Along with affordable British souvenirs, there are also interesting boutiques and some unique treasures, although most are marked at top prices. The main Portobello market takes place on Friday and Saturday (♿ *p. 82*).

Design

46 **Pedlars** – *128 Talbot Road - ⊖ Ladbroke Grove or Westbourne Park - ☎020 7727 7799 - www. pedlars.co.uk - Mon-Fri 8am-6pm, Sat 9am-6pm, Sun 10am-5pm.* At Pedlars, the focus is on beautiful pieces with a story to tell from British designers and vintage finds from farther afield. The result is a joy of a shop with all sorts of homewares, bags, stationery and gifts. It also offers coffee.

Boutique solidaire

20 **Oxfam** – *245 Westbourne Grove - ⊖ Notting Hill Gate ou Royal Oak - ☎020 7229 5000 - www.oxfam. org.uk - Mon-Sat 10am-6pm, Sun 12pm-2pm - Closed Easter and 25-26 Dec.* Second-hand clothes of all kinds, the sales of which go towards supporting Oxfam's projects to fight poverty all over the world.

MARYLEBONE

Local map *p. 87*

Fashion

21 **Top Shop** – *D3 - 214 Oxford St. - ⊖ Oxford Circus - ☎020 7636 7700 - www.topshop.co.uk - Mon-Fri 9:30am-10pm; Sat 9am-10pm; Sun 11:30am-6pm.* The biggest, and arguably most-popular, of London's high street clothing stores, with other addresses across the capital (and UK). Budget-friendly, cutting-edge designs for fashion-conscious men and women. In the basement of the store, treat yourself to a manicure at the fantastical **Wah Nails**.

22 **Primark** – *C4 - 499-517 Oxford St.- ⊖ Marble Arch - ☎020 7495 0420 - www.primark.co.uk - Mon-Sat, 8am-10pm; Sun, 11:30am-6pm.* A serious competitor for Top Shop, with more of a focus on budget.

BLOOMSBURY

Accessories

23 **James Smith & Sons** – *E3 - 53 New Oxford St. - ⊖ Tottenham Court Road - ☎020 7836 4731 - www. james-smith.co.uk - ♿ - 10am-5:45pm; Wed, 10:30am-5.15pm, Sat 10am-5:15pm.* Since 1830, this historic store has been selling the staple of any London visit, the umbrella! The store is Victorian in style, and offers a wide range of walking sticks, men's and women's umbrellas and beautifully made gifts and accessories.

Paper

36 **Paperchase** – *D3* - *213-215 Tottenham Court Rd -* ⊖ *Goodge Street -* ☏*020 7467 6200 - www. paperchase.co.uk - Mon-Fri 8:30am-8pm, Sat 9am-7pm, Sun 11:30am-6pm.* Three floors of modern stationery – cards, paper, notebooks, stickers and pens.

Design

43 **Tiger** – *D3* - *241-242 Tottenham Court Rd -* ⊖ *Tottenham Court Road -* ☏*020 7467 6200 - www.tigerstores. co.uk -* &. - *11am-7:30pm - Closed 25 Dec.* This Danish brand offers a wealth of cute knick-knacks, gadgets and household items at low prices.

CAMDEN TOWN

***Local map** p. 94*

Flea Markets

25 **Camden Markets** – *Chalk Farm Rd -* ⊖ *Camden Town - www. camdenmarket.com - 10am-6pm.* While most shops are open during the week, it is the weekend when the streets come alive with the markets. Now a huge operation with vast number of stalls, some of the original charm has been lost, but it is worth a wander nontheless. In particular check out the Stables Antique Market, housed in the old stables (& *p. 93).*

Fashion

35 **Cyberdog** – *Stables Market, Chalk Farm Rd -* ⊖ *Camden Town -* ☏*0207 482 2842 - www.cyberdog.net -* &. - *11am-7:30pm - Closed 25 Dec.* Neon-lit, with pumping electronic music, this club-meets-shopping experience is for those looking for futuristic designs, rave-ware, cyber-style fashions and naughty accessories.

EAST END

***Local map** p. 98-99*

Markets

27 **Old Spitalfields Market** – *H3* - *Inbetween Commercial St. and Brushfield St. -* ⊖ *Liverpool Street -* ☏*020 7377 1496 - www.spitalfields. co.uk - Shops, 10am-7pm; restarants, Mon-Fri 8am-11pm, Sat-Sun 9am-11pm.* No market on Monday and Saturday, but the shops are open. In this old restored hall, you can find designer clothes at affordable prices, jewellery, vintage decorations and home and design stores (& *p. 100).*

29 **Columbia Road Flower Market** – *H2* - *Columbia Rd -* ⊖ *Hoxton (Overground) - www.columbiaroad. info - Sun 8am-3pm.* This flower market has undergone a revival since East London became the hip neighbourhood it is today. There are colourful and interesting craft shops all along the north and south side of the street, as well as galleries, cafes and restaurants. Tip: come early to avoid the crowds.

42 **Boxpark Shoreditch** – *H2* - *2-10 Bethnal Green Rd -* ⊖ *Shoreditch High Street (Overground) -* ☏*020 7033 2899 - www.boxpark.co.uk -* &. - *11am-11pm - Closed 25-26 Dec, 1 Jan.* About sixty shipping containers have been converted to house cool fashion brands both well-known and new, and independent restaurants, some of them on the roof terrace.

Boxpark

© Patrice Hauser/hemis.fr

Fashion

30 Absolute Vintage – *H3* - 15 Hanbury St. - ⊖ Shoreditch High Street (Overground) or Liverpool Street - ☏020 7247 3883 - www. absolutevintage.co.uk - ♿ - 11am-7pm - Closed 25 Dec. A vintage shoe-lover's paradise, with hundreds of pairs in all kinds of styles. There are some great finds, but you have to be prepared for a good rummage. Also handbags, accessories and clothing for men and women.

31 Sunday Upmarket – *H3* - Old Truman Brewery - 91 Brick Lane - ⊖ Shoreditch High Street (Overground) - ☏020 7770 6028 - www.sundayupmarket.co.uk - Sun 10am-6pm. Located in the courtyard of an old brewery (♿ p. 100), this vast warehouse welcomes young designers, second-hand clothes sellers and world and organic food stalls. A great place for cheap, interesting eats.

47 Beyond Retro – 110-112 Cheshire St. - ⊖ Shoreditch High Street (Overground) - ☏020 7729 9001 - www.beyondretro.com - ♿ - Mon-Sat 10am-7pm (Thur 8pm), Sun 11:30am-6pm - Closed 25-26 Dec. One of the temples of vintage London. This gigantic hangar brings together clothes and accessories for men and women from the 1920s to 1990s.

Music

33 Rough Trade East – *H3* - Old Truman Brewery - 91 Brick Lane - ⊖ Shoreditch High Street (Overground) or Aldgate East - ☏020 7392 7788 - www.roughtrade.com - ♿ - Mon-Thur 8am-9pm, Fri 8am-8pm, Sat 10am-8pm, Sun 11am-7pm - Closed 25-26 Dec, 1 Jan. An independent record store. Knowledgeable and helpful staff are on hand to guide you.

Deco

48 Jimbobart – *H2* - 24 Cheshire St. - ⊖ Shoreditch High Street (Overground) - ☏020 7739 7565 - www.jimbobart.com - 11am-5pm. The pleasing, stylised animals of the illustrator James Ward, alias Jimbobart, all have a humorous story to tell – Mr Racoon loves macaroons, and the apes in capes only eat grapes. Allegedly. Collect art prints, cushions, stationery, plates and cups.

Nightlife

London never sleeps.
Pubs (&*p. 128*) are always popular in the early evening. The trendy bars of Soho, Clerkenwell, Islington and the East End come alive later into the night, attracting a younger clientele. Many of these have live music or DJs and dancing can go on until the early hours. Late-night bars offer a more economical night out than clubs, which often have high entrance fees and where the party doesn't usually begin until around midnight.

You can also spend an evening at the theatre or concert. There are a huge number of musicals and shows (&*p. 178*) in the theatres of the West End. Look around Leicester Square, particularly on the Strand (Savoy, Adelphi); Shaftesbury Avenue (Queen's, Palace, Lyric, Gielgud); Charing Cross Road (Phoenix, Garrick, Wyndham's); Haymarket (Her Majesty's, Haymarket); Catherine Street (Drury Lane); Wellington Street (Lyceum), etc.

For programming, see *TimeOut* (& *p. 154*) or **www.officiallondon theatre.co.uk**.

Half-price tickets for the day's performances are available at the **TKTS kiosk** (www.tkts.co.uk) in Leicester Square.

& Find the addresses on our plans with numbered pads (ex. ❶). Les coordinates in red(ex. C2) refer to the detachable plan.

MAYFAIR

***Local map** p. 28-29*

⓭ The Connaught Bar – *C4* - *Carlos Place* - Bond Street - 020 7314 3419 - www.the-connaught.co.uk - & - *4pm-1am.* This glamorous and stylish bar, with low lighting and furnished in plush fabrics, is the perfect setting for sipping a cocktail or (if your budget can stretch to it) two. Mixologists serve up great drinks, as well as classic martinis from the famous martini trolley, always served stirred, not shaken.

SOHO

141

***Local map** p. 28-29*

❷ Bar Rumba – *D4* - *36 Shaftesbury Av.* - Piccadilly Circus - 020 7287 6933 - www.barrumbadisco.co.uk - *9pm-3am (Tue 6pm, Fri-Sat 7pm).* In the heart of Soho, Bar Rumba is a popular late-night venue. The music varies from jazz and house to funk and latino. There is also comedy on a Thursday, Friday and Saturday in the early evening.

㉑ Cirque le Soir – *D4* - *15-21 Ganton St.* - Oxford Circus - 020 7287 8001 - www.cirquelesoir.com - *11:30pm-3:30am, closed Tue, Thur and Sun* - *£20.* Burlesque, cabaret and circus rolled into one. A decadent and hedonistic party venue, with jugglers, fire-eaters, acrobats and dancers. House and hip-hop.

THE CITY

Local map p. 50-51

7 **Fabric** – *F3* - *77a Charterhouse St. - ⊖ Farringdon - ✆020 7336 8898 - www.fabriclondon.com - ᬇ - Fri-Sun, from 11pm - £ 10-26 entry.* A huge venue (three rooms) with a state-of-the-art sound system and vibrating dancefloor. It attracts the biggest name DJs, as well as the most exciting underground talent and live acts. Clientele ranges from 20-30 years old. Techno-house and drum 'n' bass.

17 **Sushi Samba** – *H3* - *Heron Tower, 110 Bishopsgate - ⊖ Liverpool Street - ✆020 3640 7330 - www.sushisamba. com - Sun-Tue. 11:30am-1:30pm, Wed-Sat 11:30am-2am.* A swift lift takes you to the 39th floor of this tower, where the bar terrace has a magical view over the City. Cocktails (£13) and good choice of sake.

SOUTHWARK

Local map p. 66-67

6 **Ministry of Sound** – *G6* - *103 Gaunt St. - ⊖ Elephant and Castle - ✆0870 060 0010 - www. ministryofsound.com - Fri 10:30pm-6am, Sat 11pm-7am - £18/26.* One of the biggest names in clubbing attracts large crowds every weekend. The sound is big and so are the queues, but a night here is a real experience. House music, garage and techno.

BELGRAVIA AND KNIGHTSBRIDGE

3 **The Qube Project** – *D6* - *191 Victoria St. (opposite the station) - ⊖ Victoria - ✆020 7485 4628 - www.thequbeproject.com - Fri-Sat 11pm-6am - £20 (price varies depending on the event).* Previously the home of clubber's favourite Pacha, this new venue is dedicated to house music, garage and disco. It is equipped with a powerful sound system, has a brilliant light show and three dance floors.

NORTH KENSINGTON

Local map p. 72-73

4 **Troubadour** – *263-267 Old Brompton Rd - ⊖ Earl's Court or West Brompton - ✆020 7370 1434 - www.troubadour.co.uk - Café Mon-Sun, 9am-12am; Tue-Wed 8pm-12am, Thur-Sat, 8pm-2am.* Renowned for having hosted the likes of Bob Dylan and Jimi Hendrix, the basement of the theatre now has an eclectic programme of poetry readings, movie nights and new musical talent.

NOTTING HILL

Local map p. 83

15 **Electric Cinema** – *191 Portobello Road - ✆020 7908 9696 - ⊖ Ladbroke Grove - www. electriccinema.co.uk - ᬇ.* Enjoy an evening at one of the oldest and most beautiful cinemas in the city. Dating back to 1910, guests can relax in front of the screen in comfy red armchairs,

© Lluis Real/age fotostock

143

Electric Cinema

glass in hand or, better yet, lying on a sofa bed (£30 £ for 2). Book in advance.

MARYLEBONE

Local map p. 87

12 Artesian – *D3* - *The Langham Hotel, 1C Portland Place -* ⊖ *Oxford Circus -* ☎*020 7636 1000 - www. artesian-bar.co.uk -* ⅃ ⅌ - *11am-2am (Sun to 12am).* This elegant lounge in The Langham Hotel was ranked as the best bar in the world by Drinks International Magazine. The head bar man mixes experimental, showstopping cocktails (around £17). The drinks menu also includes wines, Bluebird beers and spirits from around the world.

CAMDEN TOWN

Local map p. 93

10 Jazz Café – *5 Parkway -* ⊖ *Camden Town -* ☎*020 7485 6834 - www.thejazzcafelondon.com - concerts: Live shows from 7pm; club: Fri-Sat 11pm-3am; restaurant, 7pm-11pm.* One of the best jazz clubs in the capital has recently been revamped. There's live music every night from 7pm with all kinds of jazz, and also soul, R'n'B, funk, electro and hip hop. On Friday and Saturday, from 10.30pm, the venue hosts club nights, spinning world music (Fri) and soul (Sat).

20 Koko – *D1* - *1A Camden High St. -* ⊖ *Mornington Crescent -* ☎*020 7388 3222 - www.koko.uk.com -* ⅃

- Sun-Thur 7pm-11pm, Fri 7pm-10pm; club NME (New Musial Express): 10pm-4am (Sat from 9pm). This restored old theatre makes for a special live music venue. With a line up of the latest bands and DJs, guests can dance the night away on the balconies or down in the pit.

22 **Electric Ballroom** *– 184 Camden High St. - ⊖ Camden Town - ☏020 7485 9006 - http://electricballroom. co.uk - ouverture selon concerts ; club: Fri-Sat, 10:30pm-3am.* Established in 1938, this legendary music hall has seen the likes of Sid Vicious, Madness and The Clash take to its stage, and continues to welcome artists of all musical persuasions. Club nights on Fridays and Saturdays.

144 EAST END

***Local map** p. 98-99*

8 **93 Feet East** *– H3 - 150 Brick Lane - ⊖ Shoreditch High Street (Overground) - ☏020 7770 6006 - www.93feeteast.co.uk - &. - Tue-Thur 5pm-11pm (Fri-Sat, 1am), Sun 3pm-10:30pm.* The East End landmark and music destination has been recently refurbished. It has two large rooms, hosting gigs, DJs, exhibitions and live video show and regular club nights on weekends. Terrace in the courtyard.

11 **The Book Club** *– H2 - 100-106 Leonard St. - ⊖ Old Street or Shoreditch High Street (Overground) - ☏020 7684 8618 - www.wearetbc.com - Mon-Wed 8am-12am, Thur-Fri 8am-2am, Sat 10am-2am, Sun 10am-12am.* A multifunctional, social hub with exhibitions, talks, and music

sessions and DJ nights as well as a café. You can even play ping-pong! Expect a young, trendy crowd.

Passing Clouds *– **Detachable map** H1 - 1 Richmond Rd - ⊖ Haggerston - ☏020 7241 4889 - www.passing clouds.org - Mon-Thur, 7pm-12:30am; Fri-Sat, 7pm-3:30am; Sun, 2pm-12:30am.* This neighbourhood club in the hipster centre of Dalston is dedicated to world music, with a varied and wide-ranging programme of interesting acts and artists.

18 **Queen of Hoxton** *– H2 - 1-5 Curtain Rd - ⊖ Shoreditch High Street (Overground) - ☏020 7422 0958 - www.queenofhoxton.com - Sun-Wed, 12pm-12am; Thur-Sat, 12pm-2am.* A club and art gallery in one, this is a relaxed venue with an underground atmosphere. There's graffiti on the walls, retro games nights, poetry evenings, DJ parties and the odd rave in the basement. In spring and summer, the large terrace is covered with grass, flowers and multicoloured wooden tables and hosts regular outdoor cinema nights (programming on http://rooftopfilmclub.com). In autumn, a giant heated tipi welcomes guests.

19 **Xoyo** *– G2 - 32-37 Cowper St. - ⊖ Old Street - ☏020 7729 5959 - www.xoyo.co.uk - Fri-Sat from 9pm, other days according to concerts.* A well-known club, serving up live music gigs and renowned DJs and club nights on weekends. The music rosta is varied but always quality.

Where to stay

Accommodation in London can be expensive, very expensive. To get the best rates book your nights well in advance, and try to stay during the the week or on a Sunday. The most upscale central districts (Mayfair, St James's, Strand) have many luxurious hotels. The more residential areas of Kensington and Notting Hill have some charming accommodation, much of which is housed in converted period buildings. Next door, Bayswater, has some relatively cheap hotel options. More central Bloomsbury is home to slightly more modest establishments that often occupy former Georgian homes. Earl's Court and Victoria are good for simple hotels and B&Bs. The price ranges below (all correct at the time of writing) are for a double room in high season.

Booking Centers

www.visitlondon.com – Official site of the London Tourist Board (LTB).
www.londontown.com – Agency offering hotels from different categories at great rates.
www.londonbb.com – London Bed and Breakfast Agency Ltd.

⚲ Locate the addresses on the detachable plane using the numbered pads (ex. ❶). The coordinates in red (ex. D2) refer to the same plan.

COVENT GARDEN

From £69 to £180 (88 to 229€)
⑧ Hub by Premier Inn Covent Garden – *E4* - 110 St Martin's Lane - ⊖ Leicester Square or Charing Cross - ✆0333 321 3104 - www.hubhotels. co.uk - ♿ - wifi - 163 rooms. Compact and well connected, this chain of simple hotels offers small but modern and functional rooms where every-thing can be controlled from your smartphone. Other addresses in Tower Bridge and Brick Lane (East End).

SOUTH BANK

145

From £89 to £225 (113 to 286€)
⑫ The Mad Hatter – *F5* - 3-7 Stamford St. - ⊖ Southwark - ✆020 7401 9222 - www.madhatter hotel.co.uk - ♿ - wifi - 30 rooms. On the South Bank of the River Thames, close to the Tate Modern, this Fuller's pub has 30 bedrooms above. The accommodation is cosy and (most importantly) soundproofed.

BELGRAVIA

Autour from £160 (203 €)
② B+ B Belgravia – *C6* - 64-66 Ebury St. - ⊖ Victoria - ✆020 7259 8570 - www.bb-belgravia.com - wifi - ♿ - 17 rooms. Recently renovated, this good-looking B&B has a modern, clean style. All 17 rooms are en-suite and some face the pleasant garden.

SOUTH KENSINGTON

From £65 to £149 (83 to 189 €)

The Mayflower Hotel – *Hors plan par A7* - 26-28 Trebovir Rd - ⊖ Earls Court - *☏020 7370 0991* - www.themayflowerhotel.co.uk - wifi - 🅿 £30 - 50 rooms. A welcoming hotel with a modern, Asian-inspired look to its accommodation. In fine weather, breakfast is served in the courtyard. Some rooms are a bit cramped (avoid those overlooking the back and the tube station).

From £130 to £300 (165 to 381€)

4 **The Nadler Kensington** – *A6* - 25 Courtfield Gardens - ⊖ Earls Court ou Gloucester Road - *☏020 7244 2255* - www.thenadler.com - wifi - ♿ - 🅿 £30 per night - 65 rooms. Contemporary but cosy, this hotel chain aims to offer *affordable luxury*. Some rooms overlook greenery and there isn't a restaurant but the hotel does have a small, well-equipped kitchen (with fridge, microwave, crockery, kettle etc) for guests' needs.

NOTTING HILL

From £129 (164 €)

Garden Court Hotel – *Hors plan par A4* - 30-31 Kensington Gardens Sq. - ⊖ Bayswater - *☏020 7229 2553* - www.gardencourthotel.co.uk - wifi - 32 rooms. This hotel, set in an attractive Victorian building, has been run by the same family since 1954. Rooms are simply furnished and offer good value for money.

From £149 to £210 (189 to 267 €)

Vancouver Studios – *Outer plan par A4* - 30 Prince's Sq.– ⊖ Bayswater - *☏020 7243 1270* - www.vancouver studios.co.uk - wifi - 45 studios and 1 apartment. This London townhouse offers charming studios, each with an en-suite bathroom and a small but functional kitchenette.

From £110 to £199 (140 to 253 €)

New Linden – *Outer plan par A4* - 58-60 Leinster Sq. - ⊖ Bayswater - *☏020 7221 4321* - www.newlinden. com - wifi - 50 rooms. A modern hotel with reasonably priced rooms and good facilities. The contemporary design scheme fuses East and West.

MARYLEBONE AND REGENT'S PARK

From £95 to £165 (121 to 210 €)

14 **St George Hotel** – *C3* - 49 Gloucester Pl. - ⊖ Marble Arch - *☏020 7486 8586* - www.stgeorge-hotel.net - wifi - ♿ - 🅿 £35 per day - 19 rooms. On a lively street near Hyde Park, this hotel has spacious and comfortable rooms, and welcoming staff. The conservatory lounge offers a light and airy place to relax or work on your laptop.

From £150 (191 €)

1 **22 York Street** – *C3* - 22 York St. - ⊖ Baker Street - *☏020 7224 2990* - www.22yorkstreet.co.uk - wifi - 10 rooms. B&B in the heart of London in a beautiful Georgian home. A friendly atmosphere and hearty communal breakfast.

From £201 to £235 (255 to 298 €)

③ The Sumner – *B3* - *54 Upper Berkeley St.* - ⊖ *Marble Arch* - *⌀020 7723 2244* - *www.thesumner.com* - *wifi* - *19 rooms.* A small 19th Century mansion, part of a Georgian terrace, has recently been transformed into an intimate and contemporary hotel residence. Enjoy a drink by the real fire before heading out for shopping on nearby Oxford Street or a stroll in Hyde Park.

BLOOMSBURY

From £200 to £260 (254 to 330 €)

⑥ Bloomsbury Hotel – *E3* - *16-22 Great Russell St.* - ⊖ *Tottenham Court Road* - *⌀020 7347 1000* - *www. doylecollection.com* - *wifi* - *153 rooms.* Not far from Covent Garden, this is a chic, design hotel with a quality offering. Contemporary and elegant rooms, a delightful garden terrace and gentlemens' club-style bar lounge.

EAST END

From £75 to £80 (95 to 102 €)

⑤ Tune Hotel Liverpool Street – *H3* - *13-15 Folgate St.* - ⊖ *Liverpool Street or Shoreditch High Street (Overground)* - *www.tunehotels.com* - *wifi* - ⚹ - *183 rooms.* A compact hotel, with a very streamlined offering in order to give the lowest rates. This is a good budget option with an excellent location in Spitalfields. Ask for a room with a window.

From £158 to £228 (201 to 290 €)

Qbic Hotel – *Outer plan par H3* - *42 Adler St.* - ⊖ *Algate East* - *⌀020 3021 3300* - *qbichotels.com/ london-city* - *Wifi* - ⚹ - **P** *£12 per day* - *171 rooms.* On popular Brick Lane, this is an affordable boutique hotel that has sustainable principles at its heart. The colourful, carefully put together bedrooms have a hip look, with organic mattresses and rain showers. Avoid rooms without windows. Borrow a bike and head out to see the sights.

From £119 to £349 (151 to 443 €)

⑮ The Hoxton – *H2* - *81 Great Eastern St.* - ⊖ *Old Street* - *⌀020 7550 1000* - *https://thehoxton.com* - *wifi* - ⚹ - *205 rooms.* In a trendy neighbourhood, close to Shoreditch and Spitalfields, this is a beautiful hotel with interiors straight out of a design magazine. Comfortable furnishings and breakfast included. Book in advance for the best prices.

From £129 to £429 (164 to 545 €)

⑬ Ace Hotel Shoreditch – *H2* - *100 Shoreditch High St.* - ⊖ *Old Street or Shoreditch High Street (Overground)* - *⌀020 7613 9800* - *www.acehotel.com* - *wifi* - ⚹ - *258 rooms.* The hip American brand opened its London address just a few steps from Brick Lane and its many cafés and trendy bars. There are vintage photos and art on the walls, and 1950s design touches throughout. Gym, sauna, restaurant, bar and club in the basement.

Planning Your Trip

London bus on Westminster Bridge and Big Ben
© imageBROKER/ hemis.fr

Know before you go

ENTRY REQUIREMENTS

ID documents – The United Kingdom is currently a member of the European Union, but is not part of Schengen and therefore requires photo ID at its borders. For French, Belgian and Swiss nationals, a valid identity card is sufficient. No visas are necessary for EU citizens and Swiss nationals.

Customs – Visitors from the EU are not required to declare goods on the condition that they do not transport prohibited products (weapons, drugs, counterfeit goods, plants, live animals, etc.). For those arriving from a country outside the EU, any excess goods must be declared at customs.

TO LONDON BY TRAIN

Eurostar – There are up to 19 daily direct trains between London and Paris (2hrs15). There are also connections each week with Lyon (4hrs30), Avignon and Marseille (6hrs) and direct trains from Lille (1hr20) or Brussels (1hr51). The train arrives at **St Pancras Station**. Check in no later than 30 minutes before departure and leave time to clear immigration.
Eurostar – ☏0892 35 35 39 - www.eurostar.com.

TO LONDON BY PLANE

Six airports serve London: Heathrow, Gatwick, Luton, Stansted, London City and Southend.

♿ *Access to the city centre varies from 15 minutes to one hour by train.*

Main Airlines
From Paris and Brussels approx. 1hr15 flight, Zurich about 1hr45.

Air France – ☏36 54 - www.airfrance.fr. Flights to London City and Heathrow from Paris.
British Airways (BA) – ☏0825825 400 - www.britishairways.fr. Flights directs from Paris, Lyon, Nice, Bordeaux, Marseille, Toulouse, Angers, Quimper, Chambery, Biarritz, Grenoble.
Brussels Airlines – ☏0892 64 00 30, ☏090 251600 - www.brusselsairlines.com. Flights to Heathrow from Paris, Marseille, Toulouse, Lyon, Nice, Strasbourg, Bordeaux, Brussels, Geneva, Zurich.
Swiss International Air Lines – ☏0892 232 501 ou ☏0848 700 700 (from Switzerland) - www.swiss.com. Flights for Heathrow, London City and Gatwick from Geneva and Zurich.

Low-cost airlines
Easyjet – www.easyjet.com. Flights to London (Gatwick, Luton, Stansted and Southend) from many cities in France, Geneva and Zurich.
Ryanair – www.ryanair.com. Flights to Luton and Stansted from many cities in France (except Paris).
Flybe – www.flybe.com. Flights to London Southend from Caen and Rennes, London City from Rennes.

Don't Panic!

In an emergency (medical, police or fire): Call ☏999 (free call)

Loss of bank cards:
American Express: ☏+ 33 (0)1 47 77 72 00
Visa: ☏0 800 891 725
Master Card: ☏0 800 964 767
Lost property: (Transport for London): ☏343 222 1234

MONEY

Currency – The national currency is the pound sterling (£), with 100 pence making up one pound.

Conversion – You will have no problem changing your currency in banks, at the bureau de change, in airports and at some travel agencies, large hotels and department stores.

Credit cards – A credit or debit card is the most flexible form of payment. There are cashpoints throughout London, and cards are accepted in nearly all hotels (excluding some B&Bs) and in most restaurants and shops. Check with your bank about fees for withdrawals abroad, and the authorised withdrawal limit. Be sure your credit card does not charge foreign transaction fees.

♿ *Banks p. 153.*

SEASONS

London has year-round moderate temperatures and frequent rainfall. **Spring** is mild and wet (11-15°C on average from the end of March to the end of May), summer is warmer (18-20°C from June to August), although the thermometer rarely hits 30°C, and cool, misty days are a frequent occurrence. Autumn is also mild and often sunny (11-15°C in September-October).

Winter is warmer than on the northern European mainland (4-6°C on average from November to the end of March) and snowfall is rare, although rain and the wind-chill factor make scarves, coats and gloves a necessity.

ACCESSIBILITY ♿

Many facilities are wheelchair-accessible, but readers are advised to call ahead to confirm. Many ticket offices, banks and other venues are fitted with hearing loops.

See **www.inclusivelondon.com** for info on accessible hotels, restaurants, pubs, shopping, toilets, arts venues, banks and more. **www.tfl.gov.uk** publishes information on wheelchair-accessible bus routes and underground stations.

INFORMATION / PLANNING

Two useful websites: **www.visitbritain.com** (the British Tourist Board); **www.visitlondon.com** (the London Tourist Board).

Download the London Official City Guide app before you travel and visit the website **www.timeout.com** to book your theatre and concert tickets. To prepare for your trip and to understand London's diverse cultural scene, read up on it at **www.londonist.com**.

For further scheduling and tourist information visit **City of London Information Centre** – St Paul's Churchyard - ☏020 7332 3456 - St Paul's - **www.visitthecity.co.uk**

- Mon-Sat 9:30am-5:30pm, Sun 10am-4pm closed 25-26 Dec.

London Travel Information Centres – King's Cross-St Pancras - Mon-Sat 7:15am 9:15pm, Sun and holidays 8:15am 8pm; Piccadilly Circus - 9:15am -7pm. ♿ *Public transport p. 158.*

Basic information

EMBASSIES

Canada – Canada House, Trafalgar Square, SW1Y 5BJ - ⊖ Charing Cross - ☏ 020 7004 6000 - www.canadainternational.gc.ca. **Australia** – Australia House, Strand, WC2B 4LA - ⊖ Temple - ☏ 020 7379 4334 - uk.embassy.gov.au **United States** – 33 Nine Elms Ln., SW11 7US - ⊖ Vauxhall - ☏ 020 7499 9000 - uk.usembassy.gov.

BANKS

Open hours – Monday–Saturday 9.30am-4.30pm. **Rate of commissions** – The best rates are generally in the banks. **Cashpoints** – Cashpoints offer £50, £20, £10 and £5 notes. Banks will also hand out £2, £1, 50p, 20p, 10p, 5p, 2p and 1p coins.

JET LAG

London is on GMT, and GMT +1 throughout the summer (March to October).

ELECTRICITY

The standard voltage is 240 volts AC (50Hz) – all appliances on 220V will work. Plugs have three prongs and you will need an adapter to use electrical appliances made in Europe. Most hotels have adaptors to hand, otherwise Boots and Tesco sell them.

OPENING HOURS

Stores – Monday–Saturday 9:30am/10am-6pm/7pm, and often later for department stores. Most stores are open on Sundays. (10am/11am 4pm/5pm) in the city centre. Many offer late night shopping (8pm/9pm): Wednesday, (Knightsbridge, Chelsea); Thursday, (Oxford Street, Kensington High Street, Covent Garden). ♿*Addresses / Shopping p. 132.* **Museums and monuments** – 10am-6pm. Many are open daily, closing earlier on Sundays and bank holidays, and rarely opening on major holidays including 1 January and 25 and 26 December.

Chemists – 9am-6pm.
For late night prescriptions:
Bliss Pharmacy – 109 Gloucester Road - ⊖ Gloucester Road - ✆020 7373 4445 - 9am-10pm, Sun 12am-9pm; Zafash – 233-235 Old Brompton Road - ⊖ West Brompton - ✆020 7373 2798 - 24hr/24.

HOLIDAYS

- 1 January *(New Year's Day)*
- Good Friday
- Easter Monday
- First Monday in May
  (May Day Bank Holiday)
- Last Monday in May
  (Spring Bank Holiday)
- Last Monday in August
  (August Bank Holiday)
- 25 December *(Christmas Day)*
- 26 December *(Boxing Day)*

LONDON PASS

Available to buy at most information centres (Tp.152) or online: **www. londonpass.com**. Offering entry and queue-free access to nearly 60 sites, museums and attractions.
Prices – 1 day (£59), 2 days (£79), 3 days (£95), 6 days (£129). Including **unlimited transport** on all tubes and buses: £72, £97, £123, £172.
♿ *Public transport p. 156.*

Whether this card is good value for money is debatable, considering permanent exhibitions at most London museums are free.

POST

Stamps are available in all post offices and newsagents. A stamp (letter up to 20g and postcard) costs £1.05 for EU countries, £1.33 for the rest of the world. It will take around 3 days to send a letter to Europe. For more information: **www.royalmail.com.**
Opening hours - Mon–Fri 9am-5.30pm and Sat 9am - 12.30pm.

TIPPING

Service charge (12.5%) is often included in restaurant bills – if it isn't, add on 10 to 15%. Service is also included in your hotel bill, but give £1 per suitcase to the porter. Pay taxi drivers an extra 10%.

PRESS

National daily press
The world famous British press is made up of serious papers – *The Guardian*, *The Daily Telegraph*, *The Financial Times*, *The Independent* and *The Times* – and tabloids – *The Daily Mail*, *The Daily Express*, *The Daily Star*, *The Daily Mirror* or *The Sun*.

Local daily newspapers
The Evening Standard is a London-specific paper and is handed out free at the tube from 3pm Monday to Friday.

Magazines
Time Out, a listings guide and cultural review, is also given out every Tuesday at stations around the city and is kept in most major cultural

institutions. Pick one up to plan your week of theatre, restaurants and gigs.

EATING OUT

In London, traditional English breakfasts and brunches are generally reserved for weekends, although major hotels and central restaurants serve them daily. London is filled with bakeries and coffee shops where you can pick up a takeaway coffee or a croissant or muffin. At midday Londoners often have a light lunch – a sandwich, a salad or a soup, and when the sun makes an occasional appearance, parks are quickly filled with the lunch crowd. The city is overflowing with high-end sandwich and salad chains such as Pret-a-Manger, Eat and Crush, otherwise London's markets have food-trucks and takeaway stalls. Restaurant lunch menus usually offer two or three dishes and are a great way of trying the city's high-end dining spots at a fraction of the price of dinner. Hours are generally from 12pm-2.30pm and larger restaurants also serve High Tea at 4pm – pastries and mini-sandwiches with a pot of tea (p. 182).

Pubs around the city attract the post-work set from 5pm, who spill onto the street, beer in hand, before going out to dinner around 7:30pm / 9pm. This is the biggest and most popular meal of the day, and it is advisable to book if you want to eat centrally – although many fashionable restaurants in Soho or Borough Market no longer take reservations.

Addresses / Where to eat p. 114 and London specialities p. 183.

ETIQUETTE

Stand in line
Londoners take a particularly dim view of queue barging, so always wait your turn.

At the pub
Restaurants offer table service but most pubs require you to order food and drinks at the bar.

Evening dress
It varies widely throughout the city. Londoners often dress up for the theatre and expensive restaurants in Mayfair or Chelsea, where men will need a shirt and jacket and women often wear a dress or skirt, while a few central nightclubs have banned trainers and T-shirts. By contrast, in most bars and restaurants in Soho, east London and south of the river, Londoners are casual but fashion-conscious.

TAXIS

Although it is quite expensive, the London cab is an attraction in itself.

Black cabs
Outrageously expensive compared to Uber, the iconic London taxi is still an attraction in itself. Black cabs chug around the city and add to the famous din of London. You can hail them when the orange 'For hire' light is on the roof and they are all equipped with a metre, and a minimum charge

of £2.60. Rates are increased after 8pm, on weekends and holidays.
Call to book: ℘0871 871 8710 (approx £2 booking).
Uber is ubiquitous throughout London and cars generally arrive within five minutes of booking. These are much less expensive than black cabs.

Minicabs

For long distances that can not be done by public transport, hire a minicab. You will often have to negotiate the amount in advance as there is no metre. Excluding ride-sharing services like Uber, avoid private taxis that are not licensed – they should all display a yellow disk issued by the Public Carriage Office in the front and rear of the vehicle. Find minicabs on **www.tfl.gov.uk** (approx. £2 booking).

TELEPHONE

From abroad

℘ 00 + 44 (UK calling code) + the number without the 0 (ie 10 digits).

London to abroad

℘ 00 + country code (1 for US and Canada, 61 for Aus., 64 for New Zealand) + the number.

Inland calls

Any call, local or long distance, consists of 11 digits.

Phone booths

Bright red phone booths are ubiquitous around London and take coins and cards. British Telecom cards are sold in post offices and the majority of news outlets. There are three prices: Daytime (Mon-Sat 8 am-6pm), Evening (Mon-Sat 6 pm-8am) and Weekend (midnight to midnight). To call overseas, you will need to buy an international calling card (£5, £10 or £20) which are sold at most newsagents. These vary in price according to the destination.

RESTROOMS

Public bathrooms are found throughout London and most are accessible to wheelchair users.

PUBLIC TRANSPORT

Transport for London – ℘ 0343 222 1234 - www.tfl.gov.uk.

Underground

The Tube is the fastest way to get around the capital, with a network of 11 lines, all of which are identified by a name and a colour. Northbound (north), Southbound (south), Eastbound (east) or Westbound (west) indicate the direction of the line. The terminus is written on the front of the train and on platform board. ♿ *Underground map is at the back of the detachable plan.*
Always keep your ticket to hand as you will need it to exit any tube, train or underground.
Schedule – Mon-Sat, 5am/5:30am to 12:30am/1am, Sun 7am to 12am/12:30am.

Bus

London's famous scarlet double decker buses are an unmissable part of any visit to the city. An affordable and view-filled way to get around London, the network has nearly 130 lines. Get a Central London map, available free of charge at all tube stations or at www.visitlondon.com. Download the Citymapper app, which will calculate the quickest route for any journey. Sixty night buses, identifiable by the letter N followed by a number, run between midnight and 7 am, and, other than certain tube lines on weekends, are the only form of night transport. Their schedules can be irregular and you will need to ring the bell at your stop.

Dockland Light Railway (DLR)
Dockland Light Railway (DLR) is a driver-free line that services the east-end and the City. DLR stations are easily accessible to people with mobility difficulties.

Overground
This railway line services a number of stations around Zones 2 and 3 and has links to most tube lines.

Tarifs
Public transport is expensive compared to other major cities. Prices vary according to when you travel. At peak times (the weekday rush-hour commute) and in Zone 1 tickets cost more than at non-peak hours out in Zones 2-4. Children under 11 travel free of charge on buses, the underground, DLR and Overground. Tickets can be bought at all tube stations. If you are caught without a ticket, you are liable to a fine of £80. A single tube ticket costs an outrageous £4.90, so buy a **Travelcard or Oyster Card** to save on costs.

Travelcard – This offers unlimited access to the tube, buses (day and night), the DLR and the Overground. One Day Travelcard: £12,10 for Zones 1 to 4. Seven Day Travelcard: £32,40 for Zones 1 to 2.

Oyster Card – A prepaid card, this can be used on the entire London transport network (except commuter trains from outside the city). It can be topped up in cash or by credit card at tube stations or you can link it to your card to top up automatically. Or pay online (www.tfl.gov.uk/ oyster). Buy an Oyster Card for £5 and get the money refunded if you hand it in at the end of your stay. With an Oyster card, a ticket for Zones 1-2 will cost £2.90 (peak) or £2.30 (off peak), and the bus will cost £1.50. There is a cap of £10 for 1 day, £15 for 2 days and £20 for 3 days, so you never pay more than the cost of a One Day Travelcard. Make sure you always beep your card at the beginning AND at the end of your journey (except on the bus), so that the correct fare is debited, otherwise you will be charged the price of a trip on the whole line.

Visitor Oyster Card – Sold exclusively online, you can buy one before your trip (http://visitorshop.tfl.gov.uk/), for a deposit of £3 (non-refundable). You will be reimbursed up to £10 if you have not used up all your credit.
♿ *London Pass p. 154.*

BIKES

The **Santander Cycles** self-service bicycle stations are found throughout the city centre (payment by credit card, 30 first free minutes). For further information: www.tfl.gov.uk. Although London's bicycle paths are improving, biking in the city centre can be hazardous, so wear a helmet. The cycle paths along the Thames and in the major parks are particularly lovely. The London Cycle Guide, available in the Travel Information Centers, offers tours around the city. Fold-up bikes can be taken on most tube lines but otherwise bikes are banned on the underground and only allowed on the Overground on off-peak hours.

GUIDED TOURS

With a few rare exceptions, all tours are offered in English.

By Bus

Some agencies organise guided tours, others will plan a trip around the city for you. Most agencies also offer walking tours.

Big Bus Tours – ℘020 7233 9533 - www.bigbustours.com. Four tours including a Thames cruise, 24-hour ticket online (£26).

The Original London Tour – ℘020 8877 1722 - www.theoriginaltour.com. Four tours including a Thames cruise, valid ticket 24hr (£30, online £26).

London Duck Tours – 55 York Rd - ⊖ Waterloo - ℘ 020 7928 3132 - www.londonducktours.co.uk. Departure from the London Eye, themed routes of 1hr15, including a Thames cruise (from £27).

By Boat

For more details on the routes and schedules of the different companies, download the brochure *River Thames Boat Services* on the site Transport for London (www.tfl.gov.uk).

City Cruises – ℘ 020 7740 0400 - www.citycruises.com. Regular service on the Thames from Westminster Pier to Greenwich.

Bateaux London – ℘ 020 7695 1800 - www.bateauxlondon.com. Lunch and dinner cruise.

Jason's Trip – www.jasons.co.uk. From April to October, houseboat cruises on the Grand Union Canal between Camden Lock and Little Venice (45mn go).

By Walking

London Walks – ℘ 020 7624 3978 - www.walks.com. Themed walks or in a neighborhood (some in French, including one on Jack the Ripper).

Street Art London Tours – http://streetartlondon.co.uk/tours. Immersion in the East End around urban art *(street art)*.

Alternative London Tours – www.alternativeldn.co.uk. Themed walks in the East End around gastronomy, pubs or street art (in French on Saturday).

À nous deux Londres ! – ℘ 079 1025 3508 (SMS slt) - www.anousdeux-londres.co.uk. French-speaking guide tour.

By Taxi

Black Taxi Tours – ℘ 020 7935 9363 - www.blacktaxitours.co.uk. 2 hours, day (£150 per car) or night (£160).

City skyline and the river boats

Festivals and events

For monthly events, visit **www.visitlondon.com**, where you can also download the **London Planner**, free monthly, distributed in tourist offices and various places in the capital.

TEMPORARY EXHIBITIONS 2018-2019

London Transport Museum (♿ *p. 37*)
▶**Poster Girls** – Until 1 Jan 2019.

Museum of London (♿ *p. 52*)
▶**Votes for Women** – Until 6 Jan 2019

National Portrait Gallery (♿ *p. 22*)
▶**Rebel Women** – Until 1 Jan 2019.
Gainsborough's Family Album – 22 Nov 2018-3 Feb 2019.

Queen's Gallery (♿ *p. 26*)
▶**Russia: Royalty and the Romanovs** – 9 Nov 2019-28 Apr 2019.
Shadows of War – 9 Nov 2019-28 Apr 2019.
Charles II: Art and Power – 23 Nov 2019-2 June 2019.

Royal Academy of Arts (♿ *p. 30*)
Renzo Piano – 15 Sept 2018-20 January 2019.
Oceania – 29 Sept 2018-10 Dec 2018.
Klimt/Schiele – 4 Nov 2018-3 Feb 2019.

Saatchi Gallery (♿ *p. 74*)
▶**Kaleidescope: A Decade of New Art** – Dates to be confirmed.
▶**Black Mirror: Art As Social Satire** – Dates to be confirmed.

Science Museum (♿ *p. 78*)
▶**Superbug:** The Fight for Our Lives - until spring 2019.

Tate Britain (♿ *p. 18*)
▶**Turner Prize 2018** – 25 Sept 2018-6 Jan 2019.
▶**Burne-Jones** – 24 Oct 2018-24 Feb 2019.

Tate Modern (♿ *p. 64*)
Christian Marclay: The Clock – 14 Sept 2018-20 Jan 2019.
Hyundai Commission – 2 Oct 2018-30 March 2019.
Anni Albers – 11 Oct 2018-27 Jan 2019.

Victoria & Albert Museum (♿ *p. 76*)
▶**Fashioned from Nature** – 21 Apr 2018-27 Jan 2019.
▶**Frida Kahlo: Making Herself Up** – 16 June 2018-4 Nov 2018.
▶**Videogames** – 8 Sept 2018-24 Feb 2019.

ANNUAL EVENTS

January
▶**New Year's Day Parade:** New Year's parade, departure at 12:00 pm of Parliament Square (Westminster) for Piccadilly- www.lnydp.com.
▶**London Mime Festival:** Visual theatre. www.mimefest.co.uk.
▶**Charles I Commemoration:** Procession in costume, departure at 11:30 from St James's Palace for Banqueting House (last Sunday).

▶**London Art Fair:** London Art Fair at the Business Design Center in Islington - www.londonartfair.co.uk.

February
▶**Chinese New Year:** In Chinatown, in Soho.

March
▶**St Patrick's Day:** Parade on 17th March at South Bank.

Easter
▶**Hot Cross Buns Service:** Mass and the distribution of Easter buns at St Bartsolomew-the-Great Church.

▶**Easter Parade:** Carnival parade on Easter Monday at Battersea Park.

▶**Trooping of the Colour:** Procession of horses on Easter Monday in Battersea Park - www.lhhp.co.uk.

End of March-beginning of April
▶**Oxford-Cambridge Boat Race:** Since 1829, the universities of Oxford and Cambridge compete in a rowing race on the Thames. http://theboatraces.org.

April
▶**London Marathon:** between the Docklands and Westminster - www. virginmoneylondonmarathon.com.

May
▶**Boishakhi Mela:** The Bengali New Year is celebrated on Brick Lane and at Victoria Park - www.boishakhimela.org.

▶**London Photo Festival:** Across the city - www.londonphotofestival.org.

▶**Oak Apple Day Parade:** Parade of the Royal Hospital of Chelsea (29 may).

▶**Open Air Theatre:** Beginning of the outdoor theatre season at Regent's Park - www.openairtheatre.org.

▶**RHS Chelsea Flower Show:** At the Royal Hospital Chelsea - www.rhs.org.uk.

▶**State Opening of Parliament:** The opening ceremony of Parliament by the Queen at Westminster Palace.

▶**Vaisakhi (Baisakhi):** Dances and songs of the Punjab to celebrate the Sikh New Year on Trafalgar Square.

June
▶**Trooping the Colour:** Parade on the occasion of the Queen's birthday.

▶**Horse Guards Parade**, Whitehall (2nd Saturday).

▶**Hampton Court Festival:** Concerts of all kinds at the Hampton Courthouse - www. hamptoncourtpalacefestival.com.

▶**Open Garden Squares Weekend:** 200 public and private gardens in celebration - www.opensquares.org.

Wimbledon Tennis Championships (2 weeks) - www.wimbledon.org.

▶**Greenwich + Docklands International Festival:** Concerts, performances, open-air theatre - www.festival.org.

▶**Pride in London** (one week)**:** - http://prideinlondon.org.

▶**London Festival of Architecture:** Guided tours throughout the city during the month - www. londonfestivalofarchitecture.org.

© Travel Pix Collection/age fotostock

Notting Hill Carnival

June-August
▶**Royal Academy Summer Exhibition:** Royal Academy of Arts Summer Show (mid-June to late August) at Burlington House (Piccadilly) -
www.royalacademy.org.uk.

July
▶**Wireless Festival:** Major urban music festival at Finsbury Park.
http://wirelessfestival.co.uk.
▶**RHS Hampton Court Palace Flower Show:** www.rhs.org.uk.
▶**The Proms:** Classical music at the Royal Albert Hall (until September) -
www.bbc.co.uk/proms.

▶**Doggett Coat and Badge Race:** Rowing races between the bridges of London and Chelsea.
▶**Prudential Ride London:** Cycling events around the bike.
www.prudentialridelondon.co.uk.

August
▶**Hampstead Heath Fair:** Festival and fair since 1850 (last weekend).
▶**Notting Hill Carnival:** Major West London carnival, centred around Portobello Road (last weekend).

September
▶**Open House London:** National Heritage Days -
www.openhouselondon.org.uk.
▶**The London Design Festival:** Events throughout the city -
www.londondesignfestival.com.
▶**Totally Thames:** Artistic events on the banks of the Thames, between Westminster Bridge and Tower Bridge- http://totallythames.org.
▶**Goldsmiths' Fair:** Goldsmiths' Hall (St Paul's), from the end of September to the beginning of October.
www.goldsmithsfair.co.uk.
▶**Pearly Kings and Queens Harvest Festival:** Harvest Festival, the Pearly Kings and Queens parade from the Guildhall to St Mary-le-Bow Church. Participants wear traditional costume.
www.pearlysociety.co.uk.

October
▶**Michaelmas Law Term:** Opening of the judicial session at Westminster Abbey.

▶**Trafalgar Day Parade:** Parade for the commemoration of the Battle of Trafalgar, from Trafalgar Square (21).
▶**London Film Festival:** National Film Theatre - www.bfi.org.uk.
▶**London Restaurant Festival:** Special menus and entertainment in many restaurants of the capital. www.londonrestaurantfestival.com.

November
▶**Bonfire Night:** Fireworks in the main parks of the city (5) - www.bonfirenight.net.
▶**London Jazz Festival** (10 days)**:** in the city - www.efglondonjazz festival.org.uk.
▶**London to Brighton Veteran Car Run:** Vintage car race from Hyde Park (1st Sunday) - www.vccofgb.co.uk/lontobri.
▶**Lord Mayor's Show:** Lord Mayor parade in the City (2nd Saturday). https://lordmayorsshow.london.
▶**Remembrance Day Service & Parade:** Day of remembrance, ceremony at the Cenotaph of Whitehall (Sunday near November 11).
▶**Turning on the Christmas Lights:** Regent Street in mid-November.

December
▶**Christmas lights, illuminations, and church festivities.**
▶**Trafalgar Square Christmas Tree:** Installation of the Christmas tree given to London by the Norwegians.
▶**Spitalfields Winter Festival:** Classical, baroque and contemporary music in Spitalfields - www.spitalfieldsmusic.org.uk.

▶**Winter W**
Gigantic Ch
in Hyde Par
wonderland

ART GALLE

Some partic
among Lond

East London
▶**Whitechapel Gallery** – ♿ *p. 101.*

St James's
▶ **White Cube** – 25-26 Mason's Yard (Off Duke Street) ⊖ Piccadilly Circus - http://whitecube.com. Other address: 144-152 Bermondsey Street - ⊖ Bermondsey.

Chelsea
▶**Saatchi Gallery** – ♿ *p. 74.*

Kensington
▶**Serpentine Gallery** – ♿ *p. 80.*

Soho
▶**The Photographer's Gallery** – 16-18 Ramillies St. - ⊖ Oxford Circus - http://thephotographersgallery. org.uk.

The City
▶ **Barbican Art Gallery** – Barbican Centre - Silk St. - ⊖ Barbican - www.barbican.org.uk.

163

Find Out More

Horse Guards
© Eurasia Press/Photononstop

Key dates

43 – Foundation of the *Roman Londinium*.
2 – Construction of the Roman wall.
5. – The Romans evacuate the city.
8-10. – Viking raids and invasions.
1065 – Opening of **Westminster Abbey**.
1066 – Norman invasion: defeat of the troops of Harold II at Hastings and coronation of William I.
1067–97 – Construction of the **Tower of London**.
1157 – IInstallation of the merchants of the Hanse in the **City** of London.
1192 – Election of the first Mayor of the City, Henry Fitzailwin.
1209 – **London Bridge**, the first of stone, replaces the Roman bridge.
1216 – The barons force King John Landless to ratify the **Magna Carta**, the foundation of English institutions.
1349 – The Black Death devastates London.
1530–32 – Construction of **St James's Palace**.
1536–39 – **Reformation**: separation of the English Church with the Papacy.
1555 – Brief restoration of Catholicism: 300 Protestants perish at the stake at Smithfield.
1558 – Re-establishment of the English Protestant Church with the arrival on the throne of Elizabeth I.
1567 – Creation of the first **Stock Exchange**.
1599 – Inauguration of **Globe Theatre** in Southwark.
1600 – Creation of the British East India Company.

1642 – Beginning of the Civil War. Cavaliers (royalists) and Roundheads (parliamentarians) clash.
1649 – Execution of **Charles I** on Januar 30, in front of Whitehall.
1649-60 – Republic formed, known as the Commonwealth of England, Scotland and Ireland.
1653 – **Cromwell** becomes Lord-Protector of the Commonwealth.
1655 – Resettlement of Jewish people in England, banned since 13C.
1660 – Restoration: King Charles II authorises theatrical performances at **Covent Garden**.
1665 – **Great Plague** kills nearly 100,000 of London's population of about 460,000.
1666 – **The Great Fire** and the birth of the first London **newspaper**.
1666-1723 – Reconstruction by Christopher Wren of **St. Paul's Cathedral** and the City's churches
1685 – Louis XIV revokes the Edict of Nantes and French Huguenots come to England.
1688 – Civil War: exile of James II and the throne is passed to **William of Orange**.
1750 – Construction of **Westminster Bridge**.
1753 – Foundation of the **British Museum**.
1756-63 – War of Seven Years which sets Great Britain and Prussia against France and Austria.
1812 – John Nash designs and builds **Regent Street**.
1824 – Opening of the **National Gallery**.

1835-60 – Reconstruction of Westminster Palace (Houses of Parliament).
1836 – Foundation of the University of London.
1851 – First World's Fair in Hyde Park.
1852 – Opening of the **Victoria and Albert Museum**.
1856-1909 – Construction of the museums of South Kensington.
1863 – First **London Underground** line opened.
1894 – Opening of **Tower Bridge**.
1938 – Creation of the **Green Belt**.
1940-1941 – **The Blitz**: The bombing of London starts the Battle of Britain.
1951 – The **Festival of Great Britain** Is organised to reinvigorate the nation.
1958 – The first women enter the House of Lords.
1976 – Opening of the **National Theatre.**
1979 – **Margaret Thatcher** becomes the first female Prime Minister.
1981 – Establishment of the **London Docklands Development Corporation** to regenerate the Docklands of East London. Marriage of **Charles and Diana** at St Paul's Cathedral.
1982 – The **Barbican Centre** opens and the Thames Barrier is constructed.
1990 – **John Major** becomes Prime Minister.
1994 – The Channel Tunnel opens.
1997 – The British Library opens. The Labour Party returns to power with Tony Blair. Princess Diana dies in Paris.
1998 – Reopening of the **Globe Theatre**. A referendum is held and Londoners will now elect their mayor.

1999 – Works starts on the **Millennium Dome** in Greenwich, the extension of the Jubilee line, the **Millennium Bridge** at the Tate Modern in Southwark, the **London Eye** on the South Bank, and the Great Court of the British Museum.
2003 – London becomes the first European city to adopt an urban toll system.
2005 – Terrorist attacks on the underground.
2007 – **St Pancras** becomes the arrival station for Eurostar trains. **Gordon Brown** becomes **Prime Minister.**
2008 – The Financial Crisis hits.
2010 – Return of the **Conservative Party** to power: David Cameron becomes Prime Minister.
2011 – Kate Middleton and Prince William marry. Violent demonstrations against austerity plan.
2012 – London hosts the **Olympics** and celebrates the Diamond Jubilee, marking 60 years of Elizabeth II's reign.
2013 – Opening of the **Shard** to the public. Birth of Prince George, first child of Prince William and Kate.
2015 – Birth of Princess Charlotte, daughter of Prince William and Kate; David Cameron reappointed as Prime Minister; Queen Elizabeth II beats the longevity record on the throne.
2016 – Labour MP **Sadiq Khan** becomes Mayor of London.
2017 – **Brexit**: with 51.9% of UK vote to leave the EU (London voted 59.9% for Remain).
2018 –Prince William and Kate welcome third child; Prince Harry and American actress Meghan Markle marry in Windsor.

Architecture and urbanism

London's architectural diversity is astonishing. Owing to the rich history of the city – its almost total destruction during the Great Fire and the serious damage inflicted by during the Second World War – there is a real lack of unity here. Alongside the modern constructions, there are still traces of its architectural past: from the Norman period remains the **Tower of London** (p.58), while the **Palace** and **Westminster Abbey** (p.14 and 16) come from the Gothic period.

168

A BAFFLED URBANISM

London is not a city but a patchwork of villages, each one having grown over the centuries to meet its neighbour without any order or plan. At an administrative level, the capital is torn between Westminster and the City. It is difficult today to find a neighbourhood that does not present an architectural disjunction, when many projects were undertaken without taking into account the existing buildings or environment. This leads to surprising, not always unwelcome, juxtapositions.

PALLADIAN RENAISSANCE

In England, Gothic style architecture prevailed for almost three centuries and as a result, the Renaissance only really left its mark from the end of the 16th century, thanks in part to the work of **Inigo Jones** (1573-1652). This urbanist, considered the founder of English architecture, admired the classical style of the Italian Renaissance initiated by **Andrea Palladio** (1508- 1580). Covent Garden square (p.35) and **Whitehall's Banqueting House** (p.20) are fine examples of Jones' work. Inspired by antiquity, the Palladian style is recognisable by its sober, symmetrical facades, rhythmic high rectangular windows, columns or arcades, and surmounted by balustrades, cornices or triangular pediments and cupolas.

ENGLISH BAROQUE

At the beginning of the 17th century, with the Counter-Reformation in continental Europe, the Renaissance gradually evolved towards the Baroque, a style that embraced luxury, drama and ornate detail. Architecture became less symmetrical and more embellished. In England, however, the evolution was more restrained than elsewhere; structures somehow combined grandeur and sobriety. After the Great Fire of 1666, the reconstruction of London offered the opportunity to apply the new style under the style of another major architect, **Christopher Wren** (1632-1723). Wren's undoubted masterpiece is **St Paul's Cathedral** (p.48), where his balanced mix of Italian and Palladian Baroque can be seen in the iconic building's colonnades, cupolas, and pediments.

NEOCLASSICISM

Following the footsteps of Wren, the architects of the 18th century blended his version of the Baroque and the Palladian heritage, giving way to neoclassicism, a movement inspired by the classical architecture of ancient Greece and Rome. Among them were Colin Campbell (1676-1729), William Kent (1685-1748) and James Gibbs (1682-1754) who made the church of **St Martin-in-the- Fields** (p.22).

GEORGIAN STYLE

Part of the general neoclassical movement, the Georgian style can be seen across England and began at the start of the reign of George I to the end of the period of the reign of George IV in the 18th century. Its most famous masters were William Chambers (1723-1796) and Robert Adam (1728-1792). Elegantly understated, it is from this period that classical monuments such as the **British Museum** (p.90) date. Also during this time, London's population numbers exploded and families had to be housed: terraced homes – the rows of adjoining, similar houses – gave unity to the English streets and can still be seen across the city, indeed the country, today.

REGENCY STYLE

From 1811, the Prince Regent (eventually King George IV) was in power and it was a time of major developments. Among the renowned Regency architects, Henry Holland (1745- 1806), Sir John Soane (1753-1837) and Thomas Cubitt (1788-1855) made their mark across the city. But arguably the most important figure is **John Nash** (1752-1835) who is responsible for Regent Street, the terraces bordering Regent's Park (p.88), Carlton House Terrace (p.24) and the West Wing in Buckingham Palace (p.25). Nash distinguished himself by his comprehensive vision of the development of an entire neighbourhood in London, that spanned from Regent's Park to Regent Street, Trafalgar Square and St James's Park.

VICTORIAN ECLECTICISM

The Victorian period brought a total reinvention of style. Architecture and design took eclectic cues from historic approaches and mixed them with Middle Eastern and Asian influences from the Empire. References were transformed and combined in often-outrageous ways. The most imposing example of neogothic architecture in London is the **Houses of Parliament** (p.14) by Barry and Pugin. Other typical Victorian styles include the **Natural History Museum** (p.77) and **Tower Bridge** (p.59). The 19th century also saw the construction of distinct residential districts: simple adjoining houses in red brick in modest districts or more elaborate styles for more affluent neighbourhoods. Cadogan Square (p.71), near Knightsbridge, is one of the most remarkable examples. Until the 1870s, houses and buildings embraced detailing but this was followed by a conscious return to simplicity. The Arts & Crafts movement lead by **William Morris** (1834-1896) emphasised the quality and superiority of fine craftsmanship, championing traditional handicrafts, and signalled a return to a simpler way of life.

20th CENTURY

The 20th century marked the gradual abandonment of the overpowering eclecticism of the Victorians and a shift toward more natural forms. On the continent, this movement was called Art Nouveau while in England, it is know as Modernism. From the 1920s, the modern International Style broke free from the excesses of the 19th century. The objective became functionality, and architects favoured geometric shapes, materials like concrete, glass and steel, and space and light. But England struggled to get rid of its traditional styles, especially the neogothic for official buildings. Modernism was also slow to assert itself in the realm of residential complexes; interestingly the widespread destruction during the Blitz did not give way to creativity either. The Brutalist forms of the Barbican Arts Centre and Hyde Park Barracks or the equally contested Bowellism architecture of the

Lloyd's building (p.55), which puts the ducts and lifts on the exterior, are arguably proof of this. Among this century's urban areas of note is the **Canary Wharf** district (p.103), elegant and futuristic with its glass and steel towers. But perhaps it is the regenerations of **St Katharine's Docks** (p.102), **Butler's Wharf** (p.60) or the **South Bank** (p.65) that are the most striking.

21st CENTURY

The multiplication of towers

The number of skyscrapers in London increased spectacularly over the first decade of the 21st century. Since the early 2000s, more than thirty towers of 100m or more have appeared on the city's skyline, some of which are still under construction, and there are nearly 50 approved projects of the same scale in the pipeline. To put this into perspective, in the centre of Paris the height of buildings is capped at 31m. So many additions were popping up along the London horizon that in 2007 the powers that be were forced to legislate in order to protect certain iconic views. St Paul's Cathedral, the Houses of Parliament, the Tower of London and Buckingham Palace are all among the buildings whose silhouette must always remain clearly visible. There is still room for iconic additions; the tapered shape of Richard Rogers' Cheesegrater may not interfere with the view of St Paul's Cathedral from Fleet Street but **The Shard** by Renzo Piano (2012) certainly created controversy (p.61) as the

© Joana Kruse/age fotostock

City Hall by Sir Norman Foster (left) and The Shard by Renzo Piano (centre)

tallest tower in Europe – its 310m is dangerously close to interfering with the cathedral's profile.

Green style

A building's curves, lines and dimensions aren't always conceived simply for aesthetic purposes; there are often environmental reasons behind them. Take 30 St Mary Ax, designed by Foster + Partners and affectionately known as the **Gherkin** (p.56). Its aerodynamic lines actually channel the wind, providing natural ventilation for its offices. Similarly, built by the same architectural studio, **City Hall** (p.61), is a dynamic spherical structure that is sustainable and almost entirely non-polluting due to its high technical materials, ventilating systems and energy-saving techniques. Another example is the 148m high **Strata Tower** (2010) in South London, which is home to wind turbines capable of generating 8% of its electricity needs.

Stratford, an Olympic success

Five kilometres east of the city, in Stratford, the skyline also underwent a significant transformation as the site for the 2012 Olympic Games.

© acmanley/iStockphoto.com

London Aquatics Centre, Queen Elizabeth Olympic Park

172

nearly 115m, it was designed by **Sir Anish Kapoor** and features one of the longest slides in the world and an observation platform, which looks out over the Olympic site and across London. The Aquatics Centre with its undulating roof, designed by the late Zaha Hadid, is now open to the public and continues to host various competitions.

Future developments

The largest urban renovation project in Europe is currently located on the south bank of the River Thames, opposite Chelsea. It is the new district of Nine Elms (www.nineelmslondon.com), an enormous project centred around the former Battersea power station. The regeneration of this historic building, immortalised on the cover of a Pink Floyd album, currently involves architects from all over the world, including Norman Foster and Frank Gehry, and will give birth to a vast complex of housing, restaurants, entertainment and cultural institutions in 2020. But the Nine Elms project does not stop there. More than thirty construction sites are underway or to come: new skyscrapers at Vauxhall, the opening of two underground stations and extension of the Northern Line, development of a huge food market, the New Covent Garden Market, as well as many green spaces. In short, this will be a new city within the city.

The challenge was significant as the total area, about 220 hectares, was larger than Hyde Park. To make this new centre more of a draw, Westfield Stratford City, Europe's largest shopping centre, opened in September 2011. Today, most of the park's infrastructure, now called the **Queen Elizabeth Olympic Park**, has been or is being redeveloped for reuse, while other areas have been dismantled. The emblem of these Olympics, The ArcelorMittal Orbit, still stands proudly as a lasting legacy of the Games. A playful sculpture of

The Thames

The River Thames has been a rallying point for centuries, the only constant in London's tumultuous history. The beginning of the third millennium was marked by important demonstrations on the banks of the river. Similarly in 2012, the highlight of the Queen's Diamond Jubilee festivities was an impressive nautical parade. The Thames remains one of London's unwavering allures; pedestrian and jetty bridges, as well as green spaces contribute to the vitality of the banks, delightful places to slowly promenade, soaking in unique views of the city.

RIVER THAMES

The main river of Great Britain, the Thames (346km) winds its way through the heart of London on an east-west axis, dividing the capital in two: the north shore and the south shore. It was the main thoroughfare until the end of the 17th century, transforming London into a major port, and is still an integral part of London life. It forms an important artery for canoes, barges, river shuttles and cruise ships. Both Londoners and tourists have grown accustomed to travelling by river ferry to avoid traffic congestion, or making their way from place to place by walking along its banks.

BRIDGES

Many bridges and footbridges span the river across London, connecting the north and south of the city, such as London Bridge, considered the oldest in the capital, and the Millennium Bridge built in the year 2000 by the architect Norman Foster. A new garden bridge was to be built but plans have since been abandoned (opposite).

THAMES BARRIER

A real technological tour de force, the **Thames Barrier** was built between 1972 to 1982 and officially opened by the Queen in 1984 in order to preserve London from any threat of flooding. Located in Woolwich, east of Isle of Dogs, the dam consists of steel doors which, in case of flood dangers, pivot 90° to form a watertight barrier across the river.

© Ianni Dimitrov/age fotostock

Thames Barrier at Woolwich, O2 Arena and Canary Wharf in the background

The Royal Family

It would be impossible to think of London without thinking of the Queen of England. So many of London's major tourist attractions are connected to her, for example the guards at Buckingham Palace, with their imposing bearskin hats, or the mounted Household Cavalrymen on their black chargers. Royalty runs through places like Buckingham Palace, the Tower of London and its crown jewels, but also in celebrations like Trooping the Colour, a display of pageantry and spectacle held on Horse Guards Parade every June to celebrate the sovereign's birthday, no matter their date of birth.

174

THE MONARCHY

Elizabeth II is the longest-reigning monarch in British history, and is the head of state, the Commonwealth and the Church of England. During the reign of Victoria, the English colonies constituted an **Empire**, the territories of which enjoyed autonomy for the most part. In the 20th century, this Empire evolved towards the **Commonwealth**, a free association of politically independent states. Each dominion freely accepts this status and, on the death of a sovereign, officially recognises his successor. In practice, the British monarchy is constitutional and the real power rests with the **Prime Minister**, leader of the majority party, after elections by universal suffrage. The Prime Minister and his or her government lead, but the Queen retains the constitutional right to dismiss and dissolve Parliament.

IN THE SPOTLIGHT

Queen Elizabeth II has presided over the greatest period of change in Britain's history and the royal family, its roles and its place in British hearts has evolved too. From the outside, the British view of their royal family is in many ways ambiguous. Tabloids cover royal stories with relish and high budget television shows depict their lives, while there are contrasting feelings of loyalty and frustration among many. The future of the monarchy after Queen Elizabeth is perhaps less certain that it has ever been, but it remains an important part of British culture. The festivities of the Queen's Diamond Jubilee in 2012 brought to the fore the attachment of the British to the Crown. A survey revealed that 69% of them approved of the monarchy. This was confirmed by the enthusiasm for the birth of Prince George, son of William and Kate in 2013, and his sister Charlotte in 2015. That same year, Elizabeth II broke the record of longevity on the throne held by her Victoria ancestor: 63 years, 7 months and 2 days. She celebrated her 90th birthday in 2016.

Economic growth

As a global centre, London is continuously balancing contrasts and tensions.

LEADERSHIP

As a business hub, London is one of the world's top three financial centres alongside New York and Tokyo. Thanks to its world class banks, insurance companies and investment firms, its influence extends beyond the national framework. Today, the London Stock Exchange owes much of its growth to foreign companies interested in international listing and access to capital in a reputable market place. The other dominant sectors in London are tourism (10% of the city's GNP), and creative industries like media and advertising. The City has relied heavily on creative and cultural fields in recent years to revive itself after the difficult economic times.

The crisis of 2008

In 2008 the global economy faced its most serious crisis since the Great Depression in the 1930s and London was majorly affected. With the collapse of large establishments, many white collar workers lost their jobs overnight. The British economy then entered a recession. Faced with the increase in public debt, the Cameron government announced an unprecedented plan of recovery, but after an end to the crisis in late 2009, Great Britain relapsed two years later. The austerity plan and rising unemployment triggered riots across London and the UK's major cities. Since then, helped by the Bank of England's accommodative monetary policy, the British economy has largely returned to form. The growth rate was 2.8% in 2014 and 2.2% in 2015. The impact of Brexit on these figures still remains to be seen.

AN EXPENSIVE CITY

London is undeniably one of the most expensive cities in the world, and this applies to real estate, transport, leisure and food. Despite wages averaging 32% higher than other cities in the country, housing is a major problem, with the ever-increasing rent prices gradually chasing out the middle classes. As a result it has become difficult to retain police officers, teachers and nurses in The City. At the same time, three of the five of most disadvantaged boroughs in the United Kingdom are in London, as are a quarter of the unemployed. The juxtaposition of inequalities is sometimes striking, with ostentatious luxury and inner city council properties often on the same street.

A leading melting pot

The election of Labour Minister Sadiq Khan as Mayor of London in May 2016 is a testament to the city's wonderful multiculturalism. As its elected first Muslim mayor, Khan delivered a resounding victory for Labour with over half of the votes and ended eight years of Conservative rule.

Nearly 270 nationalities are represented in the capital and more than 300 languages are in use, with over a quarter of the population hailing from outside the UK.

MULTICULTURALISM

London is one of the world's most multicultural cities, attracting people from around the globe.
Immigrants from former British colonies are middle to upper-middle class, working as doctors, teachers, solicitors and barristers. Others are entrepreneurs, creatives and academics.
Many neighbourhoods are ethnic enclaves. The most populous being east London, densely enriched with African, Asian, Caribbean, and Eastern European communities. Brick Lane (&p.101), and Hackney remain cultural favourites in the east; Brixton in the south; Tottenham in the north. Chinatown, originally in the east end, remains a popular attraction in the west end (&p.34).

All communities have retained their own festivals and traditions, the most famous of which are now key features in London's events calendar; Notting Hill Carnival (&p.162) and the Chinese New Year (&p.161).

CONTINUITY

Great Britain has always advocated freedom of expression and political tolerance of minorities, making it possible for communities to live together peacefully.
As well as refugees from some Middle Eastern and African countries, a significant number of immigrants come from Eastern Europe and are young high-level graduates who move over thanks to the freedom to work.
An divisive political issue in the UK is the cost and benefits of mass migration, a debate that ultimately led to Brexit.
By 2015, the United Kingdom had a net migration of 330,000, of whom 184,000 were Europeans. This figure was taken by the supporters of Brexit, who won by 51.9% in the referendum of 23 June 2016.
Note that liberal-leaning London voted 75.3% Remain. In broad terms, the younger and more educated the voter, the more likely they voted Remain.

The East End

COCKNEY FAMED

Often seen as a symbol of real London, a true Cockney will have been born within hearing distance of the sound of the bells of St Mary-le-Bow church in Cheapside. In practice, this encompasses all the inhabitants of the East End but especially the neighbourhoods of Spitalfields, Bethnal Green, Stepney, Shoreditch, Whitechapel, Finsbury, Hackney, Wapping, Limehouse, Poplar, Millwall, Bow and Mile End.

ALL ABOUT COMMUNITY

Cockneys are known for their friendliness, their sense of solidarity and camaraderie, for being good neighbours and for their great sense of humour. The neighbourhoods centre around local pubs, where everyone meets after work for a cold pint and catch up. The long-running television series East Enders, broadcasted since 1985, celebrates the Cockney community, united around large families and strong relationships. Of course, the Cockney accent can be a bit tricky to understand, and in the past they were often looked down upon by those who spoke the Queen's English, but there is an overwhelming charm in their banter and colourful expressions.

PEARLY KINGS AND QUEENS

The Pearly Kings and Queens are an organised charitable tradition of Cockney culture in London. They wear intricate, handmade costumes embroidered with mother-of-pearl buttons; a single suit can consist of thousands of buttons and weigh over 30kg. Each district elects its king and queen and it is customary for pearlies in costume to parade during major celebrations, including the Pearly Harvest Festival in September.

© Grant Rooney/age fotostock

Pearly King entertaining the crowd

The West End

Since capturing the collective imagination in the day of William Shakespeare five centuries ago, theatre has been an integral part of London life, remaining one of the great British cultural constants. Following in the footsteps of Shakespeare and Marlowe, playwrights such as Ben Johnson (1572-1637), Thomas Sheridan (1719-1788), Oscar Wilde (1854-1900) and George Bernard Shaw (1856-1950) have ensured that the British dramatic tradition is second to none, taking audiences on unforgettable journeys of human experience. Today, Alan Ayckbourn, Edward Bond and Tom Stoppard are among the foremost British playwrights and theatre culture remains more popular than ever.

THEATRE

In 1963, the National Theatre Company was created to produce original works that could not be played in West End theatres (p.141) in response to commercial pressures. The 1990s saw the revival of great classics asserting themselves and community works created, while at the same time, underground theatre started to spread, taking on controversial and provocative themes. This subversive scene enabled many famous authors to produce their most experimental works, younger ones to meet their audience and to confront the critics, and new actors to explore their talent. The most famous homes of new theatre are the Bush Theatre at Shepherd's Bush, King's Head at Islington and the Battersea Arts Centre at Clapham.

MUSICALS

Since the 1960s, the musical has been one of the biggest draws of the London West End. The plays skilfully combine drama, comedy, pathos and romance, with music and dance. You can't talk about London's musicals and not mention Andrew Lloyd Webber, who has become one of the most successful and prolific composers of the genre. His shows have run for years in the West End theatres and on Broadway in New York. He produced Evita, The Phantom of the Opera, Cats, Jesus Christ Superstar, The Woman in White and most recently School of Rock to name but a few. Another successful producer, Cameron Mackintosh launched Les Misérables and Mary Poppins. The list of famous musicals is almost endless; Oh! Calcutta!, Grease, The King and I, The Lion King and Wicked, Roald Dahl's Matilda and Charlie and the Chocolate Factory, which are a hit for both young and old alike, and the newest musical phenomenon Hamilton.
Now you can make your choice!

Pop music

Born in the US in the 1950s, rock and roll became the musical staple in Europe in the 1960s, where it was quickly revolutionised in swinging London into pop music.

PIONEERS

London was the site of many hysterical scenes based on two iconic bands. On the one hand, you had the Rolling Stones. Led by Mick Jagger, they were rebellious and exciting, making their debut at the Ealing Club in 1962 with an attitude and sound that arguably did more to define the rock and roll genre than any other band in history. On the other hand, the Beatles, formed in 1960 and originally from Liverpool. Constantly surrounded by screaming fans, they completely revolutionised popular music and became one of the most influential bands of the century. Both bands were groundbreaking and are covered in honours – Jagger and McCartney have both been Knighted – and both bands continue to divide the fans to this day.

POPULAR ARTISTS

Music continued to evolve into the 1970s. Pink Floyd's experimental, progressive and psychedelic music broke free of conventional pop music. Led Zeppelin, considered alongside Deep Purple to be one of the major influencers of heavy metal, in many ways, culturally and musically defined the '70s. It is also the decade of big

shows and glam rock, with the likes of Queen, Genesis, Elton John and David Bowie taking elaborate statecraft to the next level.

PUNK

By 1976, pop reigned supreme, but a growing sense of social alienation and anger saw the London music scene erupt with a new, chaotic genre: punk. Few bands embody this movement like the Sex Pistols who shook and shocked the nation with songs like Anarchy in the UK and God Save the Queen, lead singer Johnny Rotten irreverent and mutinous to the last. The punk movement was followed by the post-punk and new wave movements, where bands like The Cure, The Police and Depeche Mode brought punk, disco, mod and electronic styles together.

BRITISH POP TODAY

The 1990s brought with it the emergence of the britpop sound, with groups such as Blur, Oasis and Radiohead influenced by rock traditions. The icons of today are exceedingly varied: taking influence from past decades, they have carved their own niches, with artists like Amy Winehouse (1983-2011), Ed Sheeran and Adele bringing on a pop renewal. Today, with bands like the Arctic Monkeys, Muse and Biffy Clyro, British rock has never been so good. like Arctic Monkeys, Muse and Foals, English rock has never been so good.

Fashion

London's place on the global fashion map alongside New York, Paris and Milan remains undisputed. From tailor-made, classic and vintage chic, to high fashion powerhouses, dynamic young designers and on point street fashion, London will always delight and inspire.

BESPOKE CLOTHING

Two London streets are legendary in terms of gentlemen's sartorial elegance. Princes, statesmen and celebrities have journeyed to Mayfair's Savile Row since the late 18th century. Here you'll find the likes of Henry Poole & Co., Gieves & Hawkes, Dege & Skinner and Richard James. Each tailor crafts exquisite, bespoke pieces using fabrics unique to them. The other stylish haven is Jermyn Street in St James's, known for its quality shirt-making, tailors, shoemakers and leather.

FROM *SWINGING LONDON* TO PUNK YEARS

In 1955, Mary Quant opened Bazaar, a shop on the King's Road dedicated to showcasing more avant-garde collections, including the miniskirts, hot pants and multicoloured tights that the 1960s became famous for. Around 1975, fashion had its own punk movement, instigated by designer Vivienne Westwood (p.132), who remains one of Britain's most celebrated – and eccentric – fashion icons. Another celebrity figure of English fashion is Sir Paul Smith, who began a menswear line in 1976 before eventually extending into womenswear too (p.136). The brand's classic style is characterised by colourful details and floral motifs, with its stripes becoming an emblem of the brand.

CHIC AND STREET

Britain's designers have been doyens of the runway for years. From the late, great Alexander McQueen, John Galliano and Matthew Williamson to the dedicated environmentalist Stella McCartney, who excludes all animal products from her collections and closely monitors her brand's carbon footprint (p.133), London is also home to the headquarters of Burberry, Temperley London and Lulu Guinness. On the street, London's style is adventurous, eclectic and effortlessly cool, combing local high street brands like Top Shop, Whistles, New Look and Jigsaw with retro pieces picked up charity and vintage shops. In East London, search the numerous vintage shops for clothes and accessories spanning 1920 to 1990.

Savile Row
© A. Copson/Agency Jon Arnold Images/age fotostock

SAVILE ROW W1

CITY OF WESTMINSTER

Tea time

Tea is to the British what coffee is to the French. The English are among the biggest tea drinkers in the world, followed by the Irish, Iraqis and Qataris, with about 2,000 tons of tea consumed a year per person. They drink it several times a day and in a variety of ways: black, with sugar or honey, with a cloud of cold milk (poured in before the tea or after depending on who you talk to), sometimes with a hint of cardamom or a slice of lemon. Interestingly, it was not the English who introduced tea to Europe, but the Dutch in 1610. But by 1750, despite its very high cost at the time, the British had taken tea and its rituals to the hearts.

THE AFTERNOON TEA TRADITION

Drinking tea in the afternoon was historically an important daily British ceremony but it is something only practiced nowadays as a treat when you have the time. In famous hotels and tea rooms, you can take part in a traditional afternoon tea between 3 and 5 o'clock. The tea is then accompanied by a delicious 'high tea' with fresh scones served with butter, strawberry jam and clotted cream, fruit cake, cucumber sandwiches, mini pastries and some fruit tarts. As a general rule, tea from India is distinguished by its strong aroma, while that of China is sweeter and more delicate, often served with lemon. You'll find the most quintessentially English tea parlours in the big hotels, such as the Ritz (but you have to book several months in advance), Claridge's, and The Savoy, or in high end department stores like Fortnum & Mason and Harrods (p. 126).

GOLDEN RULES OF TEA PREPARATION

The English are very particular about how tea should be prepared, so it is essential to follow some rules. First of all, in order for the tea to release its aroma, it is necessary to warm the inside of the teapot with hot water. Next comes the tea: one teaspoon of quality loose leaf tea per cup, plus one for the teapot. The hot water can then be poured onto the leaves, but be careful, it should be freshly boiled and not boiling; too hot and it will spoil the leaves. The steeping time for the leaves depends on the quality of the tea, but it should never exceed five minutes. Stir gently and serve.

London specialities

TRADITIONAL DISHES

The English breakfast

Usually reserved for the weekend, the classic English breakfast consists of eggs, bacon and toast, orange juice and tea or coffee. To qualify as Full English, it must also include sausages, tomatoes and baked beans, but will often include black pudding and hash browns too.

Main course

There is nothing like a hearty English pie. Meat in a rich sauce is covered with pastry and baked in the oven; try a traditional beef and kidney pie or chicken and mushroom pie. Another well-loved British treat is the Cornish pasty, a baked meat and potato pastry, which is ideal for on-the-go dining. And of course, let's not forget fish and chips; breaded fish fillet served with fries, salt and malt vinegar. It is not uncommon to have a cheese course at dinner, which follows after dessert and comes with a glass of port. Cheese is also a key part of the classic Ploughman's lunch – cheese, chutney, fresh bread – a pub favourite.

Desserts

Visitors to London will not be disappointed by British classics like apple pie, fruit crumble, treacle tart, sticky toffee pudding or trifle (sponge cake, custard, fruit jelly, whipped cream and fruit).

MODERN BRITISH

The former British Empire created a culinary legacy of recipes from Southern Asia, Africa, the West Indies, the Middle East and the Far East. Appearing more than ten years ago, the label 'Modern British' came to describe the country's evolved gastronomic tradition, one that honours fresh, organic products and a refined yet relaxed presentation. Leaders such as Marcus Wareing, Bruce Poole or the media-friendly Jamie Oliver and Gordon Ramsay, are the champions of this innovative and well-respected movement. Since the early 2000s, chefs have increasingly fallen for the experimental nature of street food and 'pop-up' restaurants. To stay on top of these ever-changing pop-ups, check social media as well as media outlets like Taste of London (http://london. tastefestivals.com), the Foodies (www.foodiesfestival. com), the London Restaurant Festival (www. londonrestaurantfestival. com), or the night markets of Street Feast (www. streetfeastlondon.com). *streetfeastlondon.com*).

INDEX

Maps

Inside

Cover

Photo credits

short-stay

◆ Charleston

◆ London

◆ New Orleans

◆ New York

◆ Paris

Visit your preferred bookseller for the short-stay
series, plus Michelin's comprehensive range
of Green Guides, maps, and famous red-cover
Hotel and Restaurant guides.

THEGREENGUIDE short-stays **London**

Editorial Director	Cynthia Ochterbeck
Editor	Sophie Friedman
Translator	Alexandra Shelton
Production Manager	Natasha George
Cartography	Peter Wrenn, Nicolas Breton
Picture Editor	Yoshimi Kanazawa
Interior Design	Laurent Muller
Layout	Natasha George

Contact Us

Michelin Travel and Lifestyle North America
One Parkway South
Greenville, SC 29615
USA
travel.lifestyle@us.michelin.com

Michelin Travel Partner
Hannay House
39 Clarendon Road
Watford, Herts WD17 1JA
UK
✆01923 205240
travelpubsales@uk.michelin.com
www.viamichelin.co.uk

Special Sales

For information regarding bulk sales,
customized editions and premium sales,
please contact us at:
travel.lifestyle@us.michelin.com

Tell us
what you think
about our products.

Give us your opinion:

satisfaction.michelin.com

Michelin Travel Partner

Société par actions simplifiées au capital de 11 288 880 EUR
27 cours de l'Ile Seguin - 92100 Boulogne Billancourt (France)
R.C.S. Nanterre 433 677 721

No part of this publication may be reproduced in any form
without the prior permission of the publisher.

© Michelin Travel Partner
ISBN 978-2-067230-23-1
Printed: April 2018
Printer: GEER